THE GOLDEN APPLE

THE

WRITTEN BY John Latouche

THE MUSIC COMPOSED BY Jerome Moross

GOLDEN APPLE

A MUSICAL IN TWO ACTS

RANDOM HOUSE · NEW YORK

Frontispiece photograph by Fred Fehl
Photographs facing pages 42 and 54 by Charles Sherman

FOR ALICE BOUVERIE

THE GOLDEN APPLE was first presented by T. Edward Hambleton and Norris Houghton at the Phoenix Theatre in New York on March 11, 1954, with the following cast:

HELEN : Kaye Ballard

LOVEY MARS : Bibi Osterwald

MRS. JUNIPER : Geraldine Viti

MISS MINERVA OLIVER : Portia Nelson

MOTHER HARE : Nola Day

PENELOPE : Priscilla Gillette

MENELAUS : Dean Michener

THE HEROES

CAPTAIN MARS : Frank Seabolt
AJAX : Marten Sameth
AGAMEMNON : Crandall Diehl
NESTOR : Maurice Edwards
BLUEY : Murray Gitlin
THIRSTY : Don Redlich
SILAS : Peter De Maio
HOMER : Barton Maumaw
DIOMEDE : Robert Flavelle
ACHILLES : Julian Patrick
PATROCLUS : Larry Chelsi
DOC MACCAHAN : Gary Gordon

ULYSSES : Stephen Douglass

THERON : David Hooks

MAYOR JUNIPER : Jerry Stiller

PARIS : Jonathan Lucas

HECTOR CHARYBDIS : Jack Whiting

THE LOCAL GIRLS : Sara Bettis, Dorothy Etheridge, Nelle Fisher, Dee Harless, Janet Hayes, Lois McCauley, Ann Needham, Joli Roberts, Jere Stevens, Tao Strong, Helen Ahola
THE LOCAL BOYS : Santo Anselmo, Bob Gay, Charles Post, Arthur Schoep

Directed by NORMAN LLOYD

Choreography by HANYA HOLM

Musical Director HUGH ROSS

Settings by WILLIAM & JEAN ECKART

Costumes by ALVIN COLT

Lighting by KLAUS HOLM

SYNOPSIS OF SCENES

THE ENTIRE ACTION TAKES PLACE IN THE STATE OF WASHINGTON
BETWEEN 1900 AND 1910.

ACT ONE

THE TOWNSHIP OF ANGEL'S ROOST ON THE EDGE OF MT. OLYMPUS

1. In the Orchard.
2. The Village Green.
3. The Church Social.
4. At Helen's House.

ACT TWO

1. The Seaport of Rhododendron.
2. The Main Street of Rhododendron.
3. Back in Angel's Roost. Penelope's Home.
4. The Main Street Again.
5. The Big Spree.

    Madam Calypso's Parlor.
      (Calypso played by Mrs. Juniper)
    The Brokerage office of Scylla and Charybdis.
      (Scylla played by Menelaus)
    A Waterfront Dive.
      (The Siren played by Lovey Mars)
    The Hall of Science.
      (The Scientist played by Miss Minerva)
    The Wrong Side of the Tracks.
      (Circe sung by Mother Hare, danced by Ann Needham)

6. Angel's Roost: In the Orchard.

CURTAIN SPEECH

Submitting lyrics to the cold scrutiny of the public eye is a risky business. Without the protective coloration of the music for which they were intended, and without the support of sympathetic interpretations, which can cover a multitude of shortcomings, lyrics have a tendency to seem flat. They sometimes convey, on the printed page, a banality which does not exist in performance. Reading poetry and lyrics does not involve the same process.

The basic difference between poetry and lyrics has to do with the difference in their functions. As a sometime practitioner of both, I shall try to describe that difference as I have encountered it.

In its lyric, dramatic, and epic forms, poetry contains its own music. The balance of rhythms, the tonal colorations, the development of the images, the structure of the thought—all these, plus those other subtle elements that make for the concentration peculiar to poetic intensity, result in a form that creates its own climate so completely it does not require any collaboration from the other arts to be fully appreciated.

The interior melody of poetry usually prevents it being set to music effectively. The sonnets of Shakespeare are a good case in point: I have never heard them in any musical setting that did not detract from the originals. When Shakespeare intended his words to be sung, he wrote lyrics—lyrics which *are* most telling in a melodic framework.

The Lord's Prayer, the 23rd Psalm, the poems of Whitman and Emily Dickinson, to select at random, are never heightened by being sung. Rarely is the original mood maintained; usually it is muted or distorted. Or else, as in Delius' *Sea Drift,* the words become abstractions in which the music leads a private life of its own, employing the poetic images as a springboard. *Sea Drift* is a work of genius, but it bears little relation to Whitman, even when the choral form allows the words to be understood at all.

When the nineteenth-century composers set works by the master dramatists, they usually had to adapt the verse-plays, not only because of the time element but also because of the poetic element. This remains true of the twentieth-century composer, if he has any intention of maintaining theatrical interest—which quite often is *not* the intention of the contemporary "serious" composer.

Lyrics are deliberately designed for music: they must adhere to a central idea, with a minimum of verbiage—except in those cases where complicated verbiage is used for a comic or violently emotional effect.

When I was writing the lyrical texts for *Ballet Ballads* and *The Golden Apple* I would carefully map out the action with Jerome Moross (our method of collaboration I shall amplify later). I then would write the scenes to interior melodies of my own devising, so that the words would be *singable* rather than *speakable:* in essence, a lyric must be anti-poetic if it is to be sung effectively. Otherwise it vies with the purposes of the music. (There are a few exceptions: among them, Gertrude Stein as illuminated by Virgil Thompson in *Four Saints* and *The Mother Of Us All;* and Edith Sitwell's *Façade.* But these

are works which create their own categories, and are not deliberately fashioned for a mass audience.)

The melodies I invented to give the individual lyrics a unified dramatic flow have been heard only by the unhappy few
nearest and dearest to me, who assure me they are among the
worst they have ever heard. Jerome Moross finally forbade
me to give tongue to them in his hearing, with an ominous
gleam in his eye that had lethal reflections. But these personal
tunes are useful if not pretty, because they preserve the lyric
line of the collaboration without permitting the script to in-
vade the usurping domain of poetry.

There is the additional surprise—and with Jerry the delight
—of hearing how the collaborator reacts to the lyrics. Very
often phrases which seemed commonplace are lifted into the
unusual by a sudden turn of melody. Even more often, the
music brings a wild humor of its own when the laughter is
fading in the script. The absence of a spoken text allows these
moments to find their proper adjustments, even allows break-
ing all the rules when necessary, to achieve a definite result.

Lyric theatre has a definite place in the dramatic orbit. The
phrase has a precious overtone due to its overuse in those Par-
nassian cliques that an actress I know describes as *"après—
garde."* But a truly lyric work is direct, open and entertaining.
It uses all the resources of the theatre in its inception.

Ideally, the composer and the author should plot out their
theme in advance with the director, the choreographer and
the scenic artist. In this way the style of the work can be set;
scenery itself can move in direct relation to the musical and
dramatic rhythms; and the integration necessary to a good
show is planned in advance, instead of being left to the hap-
hazard mercies of a quick production.

That is why scenery, movement and the varying atmospheres

are indicated so specifically in the script. I hope these indications will help the reader see what is intended to happen on the stage. Some critics, when *The Golden Apple* was performed, remarked on the debt it owed to its scenic and choreographic effects. This is certainly true, but as is evident from the libretto, I hope, these effects were conceived as an integral part of the work—leaving, of course, a free hand for each creative department to contribute its unhampered best.

The Golden Apple has undergone all the rigors likely to beset any collaborative effort in the queasy atmosphere of the theatre. Jerome Moross wanted to compose, and I wanted to write, a musical in the manner of our *Ballet Ballads,* developing the style of those pieces into a framework that could tell a unified story.

Naturally, our first problem was how to eat while putting such a long and complicated show together. Our first show had been handsomely commissioned by that dapper Maecenas of Shubert Alley, Mike Todd. (Regretfully relinquished by Mike, it had later arrived at the Music Box via ANTA's brave sponsorship.)

When *The Golden Apple* project was submitted to the Guggenheim Foundation, a fellowship from them enabled me to begin writing it.

The Golden Apple attracted me as a dramatic theme that was both timely and colorful. I set out to tell the stories of Ulysses and Penelope, Paris and Helen, as they would have happened in America. It was to be no adaptation of Homeric grandeurs, but a comic reflection of classical influence on the way we think nowadays. Therefore any myths we might use were to arise out of our native songs, dances, jokes and ideas.

For example, Ulysses was to be a veteran returning home to Penelope after a hitch in the Spanish-American War. Helen was to be a farmer's daughter, and Paris a traveling salesman.

The Olympian goddesses translated easily into high-powered ladies familiar to us all. Minerva became the village school-marm. Juno became Mrs. Juniper, combining in her person—as any proper clubwoman does—the attributes of both Juno and Jupiter. Aphrodite became the matchmaking wife of the local military man.

The setting suggested itself. Thumbing through the atlas I was delighted to discover that a Mount Olympus existed in the State of Washington.

The action takes place from 1900 to 1910—the best time to span for our story, we decided. The new century was charged with energy and optimism, and its first ten years initiated many of the main currents still important in our national pattern. This was an ideal climate for our central theme—Ulysses' search for a set of stable values in the frenetic process of change.

To bypass the heaviness that threatened such a theme, and to give it a general rather than a private meaning, we agreed to describe that search in terms of the popular songs and dances of the period—waltzes, ragtime, blues, vaudeville turns, etc. I burrowed through the files of old song hits at the public library, continually delighted by the vitality and innocence of the lyrics.

Jerry Moross evolved tunes of his own to project the open rhythms of that sprightly era. He felt that the musical flow should be continual, so that the episodic nature of the script would not seem choppy.

The result is completely different from such forms as opera and ballet. It develops out of musical comedy, consisting of what can be called a series of interlocking production num-bers. The sung dialogue, instead of the artificial recitative of opera, is rendered in short songs whose separate melodies become part of the major production number.

Naturally this took time to do carefully, but we finally condensed the work and solved the musical and dramatic dilemmas to our satisfaction.

However, we had overestimated the burning demand for novelty. *The Golden Apple* was taken up and quickly put down again by a succession of eminent producers who believed in its merits but predicted insuperable difficulties in financing a show that demanded top Broadway facilities and still embodied so many innovations in technique.

One event cheered us up during the whirl of auditions for a series of baffled impresarios. William and Jean Eckart, the brilliant young designers, turned up at one audition, fell in love with the show and sneaked away a script. Without telling us, they devised a production scheme for their own amusement, and we nervously invaded their atelier to see what they had done.

We were charmed and reassured because, working independently of us, they had found bold and ingenious ways to bring out the shifting moods and unbroken pace that our show demanded.

Meanwhile, the auditions swept on in my apartment at a lease-breaking pace. After the twentieth audition, I had the impression that my neighbors and the nettled spectators who lived across the court were about to perform the songs along with us. Finally Jerry went back to Hollywood to do the ballet sequences for *Hans Christian Andersen,* and I retreated to a rocky farm in Vermont to brood and eschew the doldrums of the theatre forever.

When I arrived I learned that my neighbor down the road was none other than an old friend, Norris Houghton. I went over to wail on his doorstep, but he paid no mind to my woes, filled with excitement as he was about the Phoenix Theater, which he and T. Edward Hambleton intended to inaugurate the coming season. I paused in mid-wail, and began a glowing pitch about the need for a bright new musical on their schedule. He looked interested, and I told him I happened to have the show right on me.

Hambleton had co-sponsored *Ballet Ballads* at the Music Box, and he expressed a similar interest in our new work. He and Houghton listened to it, liked it, and the three long years suddenly terminated in a whirl of activity.

The Eckarts adapted their sets to the requirements of the Phoenix stage. Alvin Colt appeared, complete with swatches of cloth, to embellish the cast. Hanya Holm, who had choreographed *Davy Crockett* so beautifully for us before, rejoined us.

Then the most heartening thing of all happened—our cast. Jerry and I often whiled away the embattled months by dreaming up the ideal performers for our opus. With only a few exceptions, every one we had hoped to have uptown flocked to the Phoenix to contribute their talents. The delight in working with them, and their belief in what we have done, has more than compensated for the long delays. (The belief *had* to be there, since the top salaries at the Phoenix never exceed $100 a week!)

The sprightly reactions of the critics and the public, the move uptown to Broadway, the awards and assorted kudos the show has received, are in great measure due to the loving collaboration of our cast and production staff—for this type of theatre relies on collaboration more than any other branch.

This collaboration was very necessary. *The Golden Apple* is a work that can be approached on several levels: its inner

life is there for anyone who cares to probe it, and its outer surface should be bright, bubbling and always entertaining. Any
portentous symbolism is to be utterly eschewed in production:
reality has its own aspects of magic, and it is the magic of
reality, as heightened in popular song, tale, and anecdotal
cliche, I have sought to convey.

After a last warning about the possible flatness of these lyrics
(without the support of the ever-inventive Moross score) may
I conclude with a suggestion for fireside perusal? If you haven't
heard the music, make up your own score as you go along,
and see what comes out. If you have seen the show, I hope this
text will revive fond memories—or inform you of those sec-
tions that were inaudible in the general proceedings.

Meanwhile, let's move on to Angel's Roost.

John Latouche

INTRODUCTION

Collaboration is very much easier when lyricist and composer
discover that their aims are similar and they don't have to ex-
plain or analyze aesthetic conceptions. From the first, John
Latouche and I knew exactly what the other was striving for
because we had been experimenting separately along the same
lines. Actually, it was an old quest, the marriage of words, music and movement to tell a story on the stage; but our starting
point had always been from the "musical comedy" rather than
the "operatic" theatre. We had both worked in the popular
theatre and in the more serious forms: he had written poems,
plays and popular songs; my experience ran from a Broadway
revue to ballets and a symphony. We both felt that the limi-
tations the popular stage imposed on its writers and composers
and the hothouse atmosphere in which so much modern opera
was being produced were equally restrictive. Our particular
approach to the lyrical theatre was to use the best in musical
comedy, opera and ballet forms with gay abandon, and we
were convinced that the resulting mixture would allow us
both to entertain and say what we had to say. Our biggest
problem was to overcome the timidity of the producers who
loved the various pieces we turned out in collaboration, but
felt they were unable to raise the money for them through the
regular commercial channels. It took the Phoenix Theatre, an

off-Broadway group, to produce *The Golden Apple* and then the enthusiastic critical and popular response sent it uptown. In devising the lyrical text of *The Golden Apple,* Mr. Latouche has been a wonder of wit and invention. His lines are always written so that they may be set with the greatest clarity, and his scenes are conceived so that they may be easily molded into formal musical structures. On its surface the piece is a retelling of the Trojan War legend in an American fin-de-siècle setting and is constructed as a series of continuous musical-comedy production numbers. Actually, our intention is broader and encompasses a review of many aspects of the American scene and the American dream. We always felt that those who wanted only to be entertained could come to the theatre and have an evening of just fun; but I hope that you who are going to read the play away from the music, dancing, sets and costumes will see, in addition to Mr. Latouche's brilliant lyrical invention, the comment he has so skillfully woven into the work.

Jerome Moross

New York City
May, 1954.

Act One

THE GOLDEN APPLE

A C T   O N E

AS THE CURTAIN RISES, WE ARE IN THE OUTSKIRTS OF A LITTLE
TOWN CALLED ANGEL'S ROOST. IT IS SITUATED ON THE SLOPE
OF MT. OLYMPUS IN THE STATE OF WASHINGTON.

THE YEAR IS 1900.

IN THE FOREGROUND, AN APPLE TREE HEAVY WITH FRUIT. A FEW
APPLES LIE ON THE GROUND. IN THE DISTANCE DIM MOUNTAIN
PEAKS FLOAT THROUGH THE HAZE OF A SUMMER MORNING.

HELEN, A SULTRY AND AMIABLE GIRL IN HER EARLY TWENTIES,
SITS ON TOP OF A TALL LADDER SWINGING HER LEGS AIMLESSLY.

HELEN, bored

Nothing ever happens in Angel's Roost
It nestles where the mountains brush the sky
   It has a pretty view
    But there's just three things to do
You're born and then you live and then you **die.**

HELEN DESCENDS THE LADDER.

Nothing ever happens in Angel's Roost
The culture hereabouts is in a fog
   The only books we crack

Are the Farmer's Almanack
The Scriptures and Sears Roebuck catalogue.

Big cities have wide avenues where I'd walk
Up and down and flirt with men
But Angel's Roost ain't even got a sidewalk
And if it did they'd roll it up by ten.

Nothing ever happens in Angel's Roost
With all our boys away how drab it's been
I hope they win the war
I've a good esprit de corps
But as the nights grow cold it's wearing thin.

*LOVEY MARS, MRS. JUNIPER AND MISS MINERVA ENTER DURING
HER SONG. THEY COLLECT THE APPLES ON THE GROUND AND
PUT THEM IN THE BASKET LOVEY MARS IS CARRYING. LOVEY
LISTENS TO HELEN WITH GATHERING INDIGNATION.*

LOVEY, *coming down to face* HELEN

Now Helen, you're a simple farmer's daughter
Don't disgrace the place that gave you birth
Display some civic zeal the way you oughter
It's the Greatest Little Town on Earth.

A BRISK FLOURISH OF MUSIC BRINGS THE OTHER TWO LADIES
TO *LOVEY'S* SIDE. THEY FORM AN IMPROMPTU CHOIR, SINGING
RESPONSES TO *MISS MINERVA'S* CHAMBER-OF-COMMERCE ARIA.

MISS MINERVA, *a prim schoolmarm*

Angel's Roost has its situation

On Mount Olympus in Washington
At the latest census its population
Was seven hundred fifty-one.

MRS. JUNIPER

Fifty-two
Fifty-two
Mrs. Gardiner's time is due.

HELEN

Fifty-one
Fifty-one
They're burying Grandma Robinson.

MISS MINERVA

Angel's Roost has an elevation
Of seven thousand two hundred feet
Eleven point five is its rain precipitation
Its chief products apples
                    and livestock
                          and wheat!

TRIO OF LADIES

Blessèd be thou O Angel's Roost
Blessèd be the products that thou hast produced
  Blessèd be thy population
  Thy annual rain precipitation
Blessèd be thou O Angel's Roost!

HELEN, *bored again*

Nothing ever happens
In Angel's Roost.

MOTHER HARE ENTERS WITH A SWOOP AND A FLURRY. SHE IS IN THE TRADITION OF THE SMALL-TOWN PSYCHIC: A JANGLE OF WOODEN BEADS, BANGLES, SCARVES AND BATIK. HER HAIR IS STRAGGLY. A CHEERFUL AND OMINOUS PERSONALITY, SHE WEARS A FINE TASSELED BLACK SHAWL. SHE CURTSIES MOCKINGLY.

MOTHER HARE

Good morning to you one and all

THE LADIES

Good morning, Mother Hare

MOTHER HARE

I came on the chance
We'd have a séance

MRS. JUNIPER

The last was a thrilling affair.

HELEN

So gaze into your crystal ball
And keep it cheerful, dear!
    This jerkwater town
    Is wearing me down
How can I get out of here?

MOTHER HARE PRODUCES A CRYSTAL BALL FROM BENEATH HER SHAWL.

MOTHER HARE

I knew this was a hurry call
So I'm all set to go

My Indian guide
Is fit to be tied
Something's brewing you ought to know.

SHE LOOKS INTENTLY INTO THE GLOBE AND SMILES WITH EVI-
DENT PLEASURE.

I predict that Mrs. Juniper
And Miss Minerva Oliver
Will split the town asunder
Through a blunder
Of Lovey Mars

And Helen, you'll kick the traces, dear
A man will take you places, dear
You'll leave your old man wailing
And go sailing
Through the stars.

Ulysses and Penelope
Involved in all of this I see
    Can't say what for
    He's off to war
But what a mess there's gonna be!

THE LADIES

Please tell us when the war will end
Will it be by and by?

MOTHER HARE

I'm sorry dears

Twill last for years
My spirits *never* lie.

LADIES

Oh my
Oh my.

*PENELOPE, A LISSOME BOUNCING BEAUTY IN HER LATE TWEN-
TIES, RUSHES IN EXCITEDLY. SHE IS TUGGING ALONG MENELAUS,
THE OLD SHERIFF, WHO CARRIES A TELEGRAM.*

PENELOPE

Ladies!
Ladies!
Lend an ear to me!

MRS. JUNIPER

What's happening, Penelope?

PENELOPE

When Menelaus told me I went mad
Now read to them the message that you've had.

*SHE PUSHES MENELAUS FORWARD. HE TAKES OUT HIS GLASSES
AND READS THE TELEGRAM.*

MENELAUS

Our war with Spain at last is through
They've demobilized our boys in blue

And President McKinley wired to say
They'll all be coming home today.

LADIES *and* HELEN

They're coming home!
They're coming home!
Coming home to hearth and bed!
Coming home!
Coming home!

MOTHER HARE

Isn't anybody dead?

THE LADIES, *turning on her*

You fake! you fake!
You eerie dreary fake
Today you said was full of dread
But you made a mistake.

PENELOPE

At last we have no need of you
To paint our futures black
At last the town is freed of you

HELEN, *in a flutter*

The men are coming back!

MOTHER HARE, *defiant and nettled*

My crystal ball was clouded
  But I stand upon my merits
The future still is shrouded
  You've upset the mystic sperrits
    Who'll get you

Upset you
And make my spells of gloom stick

LOVEY MARS

Go home and ride your broomstick!

MOTHER HARE STALKS OUT.

HELEN

Our lads no longer have to roam
Over land and sea.

THE LADIES RUN OFF.

MENELAUS

And Helen, you'll be safer home
Under lock and key.

HE TAKES HER OFF.

PENELOPE

Ulysses
Ulysses

As you come nearer
The future's clearer
And all that's dear to me grows much **dearer**
  My love is on the way
  My love is on the way

The air is keener
The skies are cleaner

The village green is a trifle greener
    When people stop and say
    Your love is on the way

The tunes that from the steeple bell come
    Never sounded so gay
The dancing trees are waving welcome
    As they teeter and sway

As you come nigher
A bluebird choir
Sings up on high but my heart is higher
    My love is on the way
    He's here to stay
    Forever and a day!

SHE WALTZES OFF. THE TOWNSMEN ENTER.

THE TOWNSMEN

Our noble boys in blue
Are coming coming
There'll be a hullabaloo
The flutes will play

The flutes will play
And the trumpets will bray
And the drums will be drumming
Drumming

WOMEN *and* CHILDREN, *dancing on*

The lonely arms that we've
Been saving saving

Around their necks will weave
The sun will beam

The sun will beam
And the eagle will scream
And the flags will be waving
Waving.

> THE TOWNSPEOPLE ROLL ON A BANDSTAND WHICH DISPLAYS AN
> ENORMOUS EAGLE CLUTCHING APPLE BOUGHS. A CURTAIN HIDES
> A LITTLE WOODEN STAGE. A HUGE BANNER ENSCROLLED WITH
> THE MESSAGE *WELCOME HOME BOYS* IS LOWERED FROM THE
> FLIES. THE STAGE PICTURE, WHEN ASSEMBLED, SHOULD SUGGEST
> A LITHOGRAPH POSTER OF THE 1900'S.
>
> THE TWELVE BRAVE BOYS IN BLUE MARCH IN PROUDLY, LED BY
> *CAPTAIN MARS.* THEY WEAR SHABBY UNIFORMS AND CARRY
> SQUIRREL RIFLES. *ULYSSES* IS THE LAST TO ENTER. THEY PARADE
> AWKWARDLY AROUND THE ARENA IN FRONT OF THE BANDSTAND.

CHORUS

Three cheers and a tiger
For our brave boys in blue!
Rah! Rah! Rah!
Tiger!

MENELAUS

Three cheers and a tiger
For our brave boys in blue
Now our Mayor's wife, Mrs. Juniper
Has a word to say to you.

MRS. JUNIPER

At last you're safe at Angel's Roost
We've all been waiting quite a while
To welcome you we have produced
A pageant in the latest style

Twas Miss Minerva wrote the verse
And Lovey Mars who set the tunes
And I would faithfully rehearse
The folks on Sunday afternoons.

POLITE APPLAUSE. SHE SIGNALS. THE LITTLE CURTAIN LOWERS.
THEY PERFORM AN AWKWARD PAGEANT. A CHILD HANDS OUT
BUNCHES OF FLOWERS, AND THE SPIRIT OF COLUMBIA STANDS
WITH A SCROLL OF HONOR AS *MISS MINERVA'S* POESY IS
INTONED.

THE TOWNSPEOPLE

Welcome to you, Captain Mars
With your pair of silver bars

Welcome, Ajax Finucane
The strong of arm and weak of brain

Then there's Agamemnon Nimmin
Always handy with the wimmin

Not to mention ol' Nestor Neider
A smooth talker but a rough rider

Bluey Weinerwitz, Thirsty Miller
They fought with Dewey at Maniller

Silas Protes, Homer Pickins
Made them Cubans run like the dickens

Skinny Diomede Kunkel
Made them Spanish holler Uncle

Achilles Akins known for fighting
And his chum Patroclus Whiting

And Doc Macahan who cured their ills
With Carter's Little Liver Pills

Last but not least of the foregoing twelve in
Glory is Ulysses Spelvin.

**THE PAGEANT HAS REACHED ITS FINAL TABLEAU WITH THE
INTRODUCTION OF** *ULYSSES.*

ULYSSES

This show you thought up
Gee it was pretty

Boys, I'm too wrought up
Thank the committee.

THE BOYS IN BLUE

Thank you for the many letters
You writ us

And the caps
              'n earmuffs
                        'n mittens
                                  'n sweaters
                                           'n mufflers
                                                    'n socks
You knit us.

THE YOUNG GIRLS

Did you have wild adventures?
Tell us
Fellas.

BOYS' SEXTET

Why don't you ask Ulysses?
He's got the gift of gab

The bright one is Ulysses
His instinct never misses
He's crazy like a fox he
Just overflows with moxie
When we get in a tangle
He figgers out an angle
He's smarter
Than Nick Carter
He's the one to tell you all.

THEY PUSH *ULYSSES* FORWARD.

ULYSSES, *modestly*

It was a glad adventure
The Philippine scenes were so sweet
  Them wee Igoroots

In their birthday suits
Made life just a Sunday School treat.

Wherever we went they loved us
So dazzled were they with our charms
  The folks in them lands
  Ate right out of our hands
But why did they chew off the arms?

THE BOYS IN BLUE

Oh, why did they chew off the arms?

ULYSSES

The same held true in Cuba
When gaily we bombshelled a port
  Though harsh blows were dealt
  By Ted Roo se velt
They knew it was only in sport

Wherever we went they loved us
They tucked us in rose-petal beds
  They welcomed our troops
  With their dances and whoops
But why did they shrink our heads?

THE BOYS

Oh why did they shrink our heads?

ULYSSES

Wherever we went they loved us
They cheered when they saw us arrive

They loved us so much
Their affection was such
We're lucky to get home alive!

THE BOYS

Oh, we're lucky to get home alive!

A GENERAL DANCE WITH *ULYSSES* AND *PENELOPE* IN FORE-
GROUND.

LOVEY MARS, *interrupting the dance*

Tell them about the main celebration
We're having tonight to honor them
A big church supper (by special invitation)
Only attended by the crème de la crème

THE YOUNG GIRLS, *gaily*

Come along, boys, when it's half-past nine
Where Japanese lanterns are burning bright
Gather around at the picnic ground
We're gonna raise a ruckus tonight!

CHORUS, *with responses by the boys*

Barbecue hog roastin on the spit
We're gonna raise a ruckus tonight
  If we don't get none we'll throw a fit
We'll raise a ruckus tonight

  Smell them three-inch beefsteaks fryin?
Gonna raise a ruckus tonight
  If we don't get some we'll bust out cryin

Gonna raise a ruckus tonight
  Smell that jellyroll coming to a jell?
We're gonna raise a ruckus tonight
  If we don't get none we're gonna raise hell!
We'll raise a ruckus tonight!

GIRLS, *softly*

Come along, boys, when it's half-past nine
Where Japanese lanterns are burning bright
Gather around at the picnic ground
We're gonna raise a ruckus tonight.

THE CROWD DANCES OFF. *ULYSSES* AND *PENELOPE* ARE LEFT
ALONE. THEY EMBRACE TENDERLY AS THE SKY TAKES ON A TWI-
LIGHT HUE ABOVE THE DESERTED BLEACHERS.

ULYSSES, *wistfully*

I used to lie awake
With the sky for a tent
And I felt such an ache
Though the letters that you sent
Always said you were fine
But I read between each line

The longing for me
That I felt for you

PENELOPE, *smiling at him*

Oh the hardest thing to do
The hardest time of all
Was the coming home alone

With no one in the hall
To say Hello
And How was your day?
You know those foolish things
That married people say

It's the coming home together
When your work is through
Someone asks you How de do
  And How'd it go today?

It's the knowing someone's there
When you climb up the stair
Who always seems to know
  All the things you're gonna say

ULYSSES

It's the being home together
When the shadows rise
Someone looks into your eyes
  And takes you by the hand

It's a dear familiar face
That can light up a place
And little private jokes
  Only you two understand

BOTH

It's the going home together
Through the changing years
It's the talk about the weather
And the laughter and the tears

ULYSSES

It's to love the you that's me
And the me that's you . . .

BOTH

It's the going home together
All life through!

> ABSORBED IN ONE ANOTHER, THEY ARE STARTLED BY THE SUDDEN
> ENTRANCE OF MOTHER HARE. AS SHE APPROACHES THEM THE
> SKY DARKENS AND A FORK OF SUMMER LIGHTNING ANNOUNCES
> THE BALLAD SHE INTONES.

MOTHER HARE

Ulysses, welcome to our village green
Though it's too small for you—

PENELOPE

We have no time to figure what you **mean**
There's too much work to do
  To do
There's too much work to do.

> MOTHER HARE LEADS THEM TOWARD THE FRONT OF THE STAGE
> AND POINTS OUTWARD.

MOTHER HARE

Look out, look out across the valley there
And tell me what you see—

ULYSSES

Blue streams, rich farms and forest, Mother Hare,
The way it ought to be
    To be
The way it ought to be.

MOTHER HARE, *as he turns away*

My sweet young man, you'd better look again
Beyond the mountain rise
There's something new that's happening to men
Come see it through my eyes
    My eyes
Come see it through my eyes.

SHE PASSES HER HAND ACROSS THEIR EYES, AND ULYSSES AND
PENELOPE SHARE THE KALEIDOSCOPIC VISION THAT POSSESSES
HER.

ULYSSES

The hills are bare. They've cut the forest down.
The farms are waste and sand.

PENELOPE

The bright blue streams are now a muddy brown
I see a desert land
    Desert land
I see a desert land.

THEY TURN AWAY FROM THE SIGHT BUT MOTHER HARE PULLS
THEM BACK AGAIN. THE SKY DEEPENS. DURING THE FOLLOWING

CATALOGUE, THE SCIENTIFIC ACHIEVEMENTS OF THE 1900'S AS
RECORDED IN WOODCUTS AND LITHOGRAPHS ARE PROJECTED
ONTO THE BACKDROP.

MOTHER HARE

Let accidents fill the world with woe
But carriages without horses shall go

Around the globe your words will fly
In the twinkling of an eye

In lightning flash and mountain streams
They'll find new power beyond your dreams

And under water men shall walk
Shall ride, shall fight, shall eat and talk

In the air they will be seen
Riding in a great machine

Young man, rise up without delay
And meet this world that's on the way.

THE PROJECTIONS FADE.

ULYSSES

That's all very well but will it be
The kind of world I want to see?

Will people be much happier
Or just keep on the way they were?

MOTHER HARE

The facts are all that I can tell
It's up to you to use them well.

PENELOPE SUDDENLY EMERGES FROM THE SPELL.

PENELOPE, *infuriated*

The wicked old piece! can't you see her eyes twinkling
Full of sin, full of vinegar and gall?
Be careful, Ulysses, you haven't got an inkling
Of the evil spell she's weaving for us all.

MOTHER HARE

Good is a word that fools believe
And evil's a word that the wise achieve
Fools who are good fools try to deny
That evil exists— they pass it by.

But life without evil is empty and strange
Without evil, how can the good ever change?
Without change how can any man ever grow?
Ask Ulysses. He's clever. He'll tell you it's so.

MOTHER HARE AIRILY WAVES HER HAND AND LEAVES. PENELOPE
SHAKES ULYSSES, WHO IS GAZING AFTER MOTHER HARE, DAZED
AND FASCINATED.

PENELOPE

Resist her, Ulysses!
Ulysses, she's lying
The devil's at work in her dark prophesying!

ULYSSES SEIZES *PENELOPE* AND STARTS TO CAKEWALK WITH HER.

ULYSSES, *gaily*

Up and down the continent
The century is toeing the mark
  It rattles and growls
  It grinds and it howls
And sings as sweetly as a lark.

Come along now
It's time that we were going
Hear the wail
Of that railroad whistle blowing.
  We'll dance a jigtime
  To that bigtime
Clanging banging harmony.
The century's young
And so are we.

PENELOPE, *despairingly*

God help me!
God help me!
I have married a blue-eyed man
Who can't stay put, whose mind I cannot hold.
Will we never sit beside the fire
And plan
On homely doings
As our years unfold?
Why can't you stay and let the distance go
Content with me
Content with what you know?

ULYSSES, *turning toward her*

I promise I'll not travel
Farther than our pasture track
  When my eyes
  Can't see smoke rise
From our chimney stack
I shall turn back.

PENELOPE

Oh don't ever promise
A thing you cannot do.

ULYSSES

I mean to keep this promise
My place is here with you.

It's the being home together
When the shadows rise
Someone looks into your eyes
  And takes you by the hand

It's a dear familiar face
That can light up a place
And little private jokes
  Only you two understand.

BOTH, *as they cling to each other*

It's the going home together
Through the changing years
It's the talk about the weather
And the laughter and the tears

It's to love the you that's me
And the me that's you
It's the going home together
All life through!

**THEY GO OFF. GAILY COLORED JAPANESE LANTERNS DESCEND
ON THE BARE STAGE. THE TWELVE YOUNG VETERANS AMBLE ON.**

ACHILLES

Ɩ suppose we should get spruced up
For the celebration.

PATROCLUS

I'm gonna bust Angel's Roost up
If someone don't start tellin
Us the whereabouts of

PATROCLUS AND AJAX

Helen!

AJAX

Helen!
Where's frisky little Helen?

Where is that Mount Olympus Venus?
High time that she chose between us.

DOC MACAHAN

Every night I was away
I hung down my head and sighed

When the ruby sun was settin
I thought of her and cried.

NESTOR

I dreamed I was a lizard
And crept back home and hid in the spring
So when she came for water
I could hear sweet Helen sing.

DIOMEDE

Oh you can climb the cherry tree
And I will climb the rose
How I love that pretty little gal
The Lord Almighty knows.

ACHILLES

Miss Helen is a blue-eyed daisy
If I don't get her I'll go crazy!

THE TEN BOYS START TO DANCE. EACH IMAGINES HE IS HOLDING
HELEN IN HIS ARMS.

Oh some girls are wise and clever of brain
And some girls have looks that are thrillin
But Helen aint smart and she's almost plain
  Yet Helen is always willin.

NESTOR

Oh some lead you on with innocent airs
And some hold you off at a distance

But Helen just nestles and says Who cares?
For Helen has no resistance.

PATROCLUS

You ask some girls on a hay ride
And some girls say they may ride
And some girls flatly tell you No!
But Helen says Let's go!

DOC MACAHAN

Our Helen ain't neat, her hair is a mess
She can't cook a meal that is fillin
So what is the secret of her success?
Well, Dear Helen
          Fair Helen
                    My Helen
                              His Helen
                                      Their Helen's
Always willin!

      THE SIX DANCERS ARE DANCING THEIR MEMORIES OF *HELEN*.
      SHE ENTERS.

HELEN

I'm sorry I wasn't there to greet you
When you boys hit the town
The truth is I'm a different gal
I've kind of quieted down.

BOYS

Wow Helen! Now Helen!
Helen's gonna marry, that's good news.
Hey Helen! Say Helen!
Which one of us are you gonna choose?

HELEN

None of you
Not one of you
Tarara
Tarara.

THE OLD SHERIFF *MENELAUS* ENTERS. *HELEN* RUNS TO HIM AND KISSES HIM.

BOYS

Oh Helen, Helen, you can't betray us.
You ain't gonna marry ol Menelaus.

HELEN

I married him over a year ago
I couldn't keep flitting to and fro

He's bent with age, his feet are flat
But his bank account will straighten that!
  I love him.

BOYS

While we fought on through shot and shell
He wooed and won our village belle

To think she'd take a fool like him
We ought to tear him limb from limb.
　We'll kill him!
　We'll kill him!

　　　ULYSSES ENTERS, SEES THE BOYS ATTACKING MENELAUS, AND
　　　NOBLY RUSHES TO THE RESCUE.

　　　　　　　　　ULYSSES

Hey fellas
Hey fellas
What's done is done
The best man won
You all love Helen
　But she can't marry all of you.

　　　　　　MENELAUS, *complacently*

What's mine is mine
I'll treat her fine
So don't hold grudges
　Which would be right small of you.

　　　　　　　　BOYS

What's done is done
The best man won
We all love Helen
　But she loves him best of all.

　　　　　　　　ULYSSES

So swear right now
A sacred vow

To steer clear of Helen
  And protect her from the rest of all

The men in the mountains
The men from the valley
For Helen has a tendency
  To dilly-dally.

**THE BOYS FORM A CIRCLE AND GO DOWN ON ONE KNEE, RAIS-
ING ONE ARM IN THE SCOUTS'-OATH SALUTE.**

BOYS

Because of the love we share
We hereby solemnly swear
To keep our hands off her
And to make certain sure
Nobody else lays a hand on her
To dishonor her.

**THEY PLACE THEIR HANDS TOGETHER IN A MASS MASONIC OATH.
MENELAUS MANAGES A GRACIOUS SMILE AND LEADS OFF THE
SLIGHTLY RELUCTANT *HELEN.* SHE LOOKS OVER HER SHOULDER
AT THE YOUNG MEN AND MAKES A DISCREETLY PROVOCATIVE
MOVEMENT. THEY START TO FOLLOW HER, BUT *ULYSSES* REMINDS
THEM OF THEIR OATH BY CLAPPING A HAND OVER HIS HEART
AND GIVING A BOY-SCOUT SALUTE. THEY REPEAT HIS GESTURE
AND FOLLOW HIM AS HE RUNS OFF IN THE OPPOSITE DIRECTION.**

THE JUDGMENT OF PARIS

THE ACTION CONTINUES WITHOUT INTERRUPTION. *THE TOWNS-PEOPLE* RUN IN WITH A GAILY DECORATED PICNIC TABLE. A FAIR STALL IS LOWERED FROM THE FLIES WITH A POSTER ON IT PRO-CLAIMING PRIZES. THE HANGING LANTERNS INCREASE IN BRIGHT-NESS. (THE SCENERY HERE, AS THROUGHOUT, SHOULD MOVE IN A PRECISE RHYTHM.)

A SHORT DANCE SEQUENCE FOLLOWS, ILLUSTRATING THE SIMPLE PLEASURES OF A COUNTRY FAIR WITH THE SHARP INTENSITY OF A MONTAGE: POTATO SACK RACES, ONE-LEG RACES, LEAPFROG, LIVING STATUES. THE DANCERS IMITATE A CARROUSEL AND ELIDE INTO A BRIEF SQUARE DANCE. ALL THE TOWNSPEOPLE DIVIDE FOR A TUG OF WAR. SUDDENLY ONE OF THE CONTEST-ANTS LOOKS UP AND NUDGES THE MAN AHEAD OF HIM. THEY LET GO OF THE ROPE. THE OTHERS SPRAWL ON THE GROUND AS THEY GAPE AT THE SKY.

THE TOWNSMEN

What's that flying
Through the air
Like a saucer in the sky?

Mystifying
We declare
It's a comet passing by!

Look out, people
Run and hide
It is heading for our town

Took the steeple
In its stride
It's the moon afloating down

THE WOMEN, *agog*

We see a man
He's waving his hand
Oh, it's the man in the moon!

ALL

No
No
It's a balloon
It's a bal

l

o

o

n . . .

THE BALLOON DESCENDS WITH A SWIFT GRACE. IT IS A GOR-
GEOUS VEHICLE FOR A TRAVELING SALESMAN, A RIOT OF STRIPES
AND BASKET WEAVE. ON THE BALLOON IN BRIGHT ELECTRIC
LIGHTS GLOWS THE BLATANT SLOGAN *PARIS NOTIONS, INC.*

MR. PARIS, DAPPER AND COCKSURE, POSES PROUDLY IN THE
BASKET OF THE BALLOON AS IT LANDS. HE OBVIOUSLY ENJOYS
THE EFFECT HE IS MAKING. (*PARIS* IS A DANCER AND NEVER
SPEAKS.)

HE TOSSES OUT A HANDFUL OF THROWAWAY LEAFLETS AND, AS

THE MEN READ THESE ALOUD, HE LEAPS OUT OF THE BALLOON
AND OPENS HIS SUITCASE TO DISPLAY HIS WARES.

THE TOWNSMEN

Introducing Mr. Paris
Of Paris Notions, Inc.
Manufacturers of the styles you love
From calico to mink

Situated in Rhododendron
That's the city down below
He's been specially sent to represent
The goods they have to show!

ULYSSES ENTERS AND STARES AT PARIS, FASCINATED. PARIS SETS
UP HIS VALISE AS A COUNTER. HE PULLS OUT SCARVES, HATS,
FEATHER BOAS AND OTHER MERCHANDISE. THE GIRLS GATHER
AROUND HIM, TRYING ON FINERY.

WOMEN

Maribou feathers and hug me tights
Bonnets and bustles of every size
Ribbons and ruffles in pinks and whites
Rouge and mascara to scandalize

Antimacassars and beads of jet
Elegant corsets to keep us trim

A DARK GIRL

Bessie, what are you gonna get?

A BLONDE GIRL

Tessie, I'd like to order *him*.

ULYSSES, *as* PENELOPE *enters*

Penelope! Penelope!
Penelope come here and see
This traveling man from the city
  With brand-new things
  Fur muffs and rings
And dresses to fix you up pretty!

> *PENELOPE* JOINS THE CROWD IN ITS SCUFFLE AND ENDS UP
> WITH A SAUCY BONNET. *PARIS* DANCES OFF FOLLOWED BY THE
> EAGER CUSTOMERS, LEAVING *PENELOPE* AND *ULYSSES* ALONE
> ON STAGE.

ULYSSES, *looking at the balloon*

Let's pay a visit
To Rhododendron
Let's have a second honeymoon

Let's take a trip down
To Rhododendron
We'll fly back with him in his balloon.

PENELOPE

There's so much to do
  And the weather we're having
  Means crops to gather

ULYSSES

I reckon that's true
We'll go another day then
  If you prefer it
  You know I'd rather
Stay here with you.

> THEY EXIT. *LOVEY MARS* AND *MRS. JUNIPER* ENTER CARRYING AN
> ANGEL-FOOD CAKE AND A MINCE PIE, RESPECTIVELY. *LOVEY*
> WEARS A SPLENDID HAT AND *MRS. JUNIPER* SPORTS A FUR
> TIPPET.

LOVEY MARS

Good evening, Mrs. Juniper

MRS. JUNIPER

Good evening, Lovey Mars

LOVEY MARS

That's a stylish tippet of beaver fur

MRS. JUNIPER

What *real*-looking artificial flars!

LOVEY MARS

Just look how Miss Minerva's drest!

MRS. JUNIPER

Her hat looks like a hoorah's nest!

MISS MINERVA ENTERS, PROUDLY BEARING A SEVEN-LAYER CAKE.
HER BIRD-COVERED HAT IS PHENOMENAL.

MISS MINERVA

Oh Madams Mars and Juniper
Tonight I'm sure to shine
I thought I'd bake a seven-layer cake
Just to prove I'm feminine.

LOVEY MARS

This pie I made has mincemeat filling
With their names spelt out in choc o late!
It's a secret recipe and I'm willing
To bet they'll wind up licking the plate.

MRS. JUNIPER, *smugly*

My angel food has won a prize
At every fair for twenty years.

THE THREE LADIES MARCH CEREMONIOUSLY TO THE TABLE, UPON
WHICH THEY PLACE THE SEVEN-LAYER CAKE, THE MINCEMEAT PIE
AND THE ANGEL-FOOD CAKE WITH A BRISK FLOURISH.

SUDDENLY THERE IS A FLASH OF LIGHTNING AND A BURST OF
THUNDER. THE LADIES LOOK ABOUT APPREHENSIVELY AND NO-
TICE THAT *MOTHER HARE* HAS ENTERED DURING THESE NATURAL
PHENOMENA.

THE THREE LADIES

Old Mother Hare
What you doing there?
Trying to give us all a scare?

MOTHER HARE

Very important ye be to others
But to old Mother Hare
   Ye're a mean old maid
   The Captain's jade
And the Mayor's old gray mare.

THE THREE LADIES

Ain't no way to talk to us
Why you kicking up a fuss?

MOTHER HARE

Fuss?
While the men was away
You came every day
To visit Mother Hare
In her poor old shack

My herbs and brews
You were glad to use
But you're givin me the go by
Since the men came back

It was old Mother Hare
You all turned to
And I told you what the stars
Had in store for you

And I read the sweaty palms
Of you pesky sinners
But I don't git asked
To your old church dinners

Ye're ashamed of Mother Hare
With her midnight spells
And you'd leave her to rot
In the cabin where she dwells

THE THREE LADIES

Dear Mother Hare
I do declare
We jest forgot you
All alone up there

MOTHER HARE

I'm so mad I could spit!
Mother has pride after all
But I came to do my bit
For the general festival.

SHE UNFOLDS HER CAPE AND DISPLAYS A GLEAMING GOLDEN
APPLE. THEY GASP.

MOTHER HARE

It's a pretty golden apple
That glitters in the sun
A symbol of our proud state
Of Washington

SHE RELEASES THE APPLE. IT HANGS GLITTERING IN MID-AIR.

Twill be sure to bring your ship in
Through storm and stress
If you own this lucky pippin
You'll be certain of success.

THE THREE LADIES

Ain't it a miracle?
It's made of golden wire!

MOTHER HARE, nobly

I brought it as a gift
To heap coals of fire

On your Christian heads
Mother Hare is meek
Mother Hare is meek
She turns the other cheek

I offer this
As the general prize
For the one who makes
The very best cakes and pies.

MRS. JUNIPER

That's me.

LOVEY MARS

    That's me.

MISS MINERVA

    That's me.

MOTHER HARE

We'll see.
That's all
That's all
And no good-byes.

I'm heading back
To my lonely lair
And any time you need me
I'll be up there.

THE THREE LADIES

Thank you very kindly
Old Mother Hare.

MOTHER HARE STALKS OFF, LAUGHING TO HERSELF.

MRS. JUNIPER

Look! Watch that golden apple shine!

MISS MINERVA

Obviously it's mine.

LOVEY MARS

Yours?
Who makes pies the world adores?

MRS. JUNIPER

Dears!
Who's won prizes for years?

MISS MINERVA

I don't aim to make a fuss
But certainly it's obvious
Which lady of the three of us
  Can bake
  The cake
Or pie that wins the apple.

LOVEY MARS, *tasting*

How terribul!
It tastes like wool.

MISS MINERVA, *tasting*

Your mincemeat tastes like scrapple!

MRS. JUNIPER, *tasting*

This frosting goo
Is made of glue.

MISS MINERVA

My seven layer's ambrosial.

MRS. JUNIPER

My cake's a dream.

LOVEY MARS

My pie's supreme.

MISS MINERVA, *despairing*

This social's most unsocial!

I'll stand right here
And I won't budge
Until we find
An impartial judge.

MRS. JUNIPER

The same with me

LOVEY MARS

And I insist
The judge must be unprejudiced!

THEY GRIMLY FOLD THEIR HANDS AND STARE AT EACH OTHER,
DEADLOCKED. AT THAT MOMENT MR. *PARIS* DANCES ON, HAPPILY
COUNTING HIS PROFITS. HE BECOMES AWARE OF THE THREE
LADIES, WHO HAVE TURNED TO WATCH HIM INTENTLY.

LOVEY MARS

Now here is a lad
Whose taste is refined
He also has no axe to grind.

MISS MINERVA

Agreed.

MRS. JUNIPER

Agreed.

MISS MINERVA

Young man

LOVEY MARS

Young man

MRS. JUNIPER

Young man

THE THREE LADIES

Decide young man
Which one is best
Which flavor is tastiest.

Let's leave the judge here all alone
To make his mind up on his own.

THEY WITHDRAW LEAVING THE PUZZLED *PARIS* ALONE WITH THE
THREE DESSERTS. *PARIS* IS VIEWING THE ENTRIES IN THE CON-
TEST WITH LOATHING WHEN *MRS. JUNIPER* STEALS BACK IN AND
DANCES ABOUT HIM IN HER MOST STYLISH MANNER. SHE AT-
TEMPTS TO BRIBE HIM WITH SOCIAL POSITION.

MRS. JUNIPER

If you select my angel food
Dear Paris, I assure you
I will direct the public mood
Until they all adore you

As Mayor's wife I set the styles
For all the local gentry
To buy your wares they'll flock for miles
They'll triple each double entry!

SHE COYLY FLUTTERS OFF AS *MISS MINERVA* ERUPTS ON STAGE
TO MAKE HER OFFER.

MISS MINERVA

I'll teach you
O such clever things
Your head I'll fill with learning

Oh choose choose
My tasty cake
I'll make you subtle as a python snake

You'll be, my love
The envy of a Harvard graduate
Just say that you are glad you ate
My elegant seven layer

You'll end up as a mayor
                    Or maybe governor
                                    Or maybe you'll be
President!

Just favor me
And you will see
That wisdom
Is heaven sent!

MISS *MINERVA* FLIES OFF AS HYSTERICALLY AS SHE ENTERED.
PARIS IS STARTLED BY THE COOING OF *LOVEY MARS,* WHOSE
ENTRANCE HE HAD NOT NOTICED. SHE DANCES IN WHAT SHE
CONSIDERS TO BE A SEDUCTIVE MANNER, COPIED FROM A
VAUDEVILLE SHOW SHE SAW ONCE DOWN IN RHODODENDRON.
SHE CARRIES A KEY, A LUCKY PIECE, TO BRIBE HIM.

LOVEY MARS

The loveliest things in life
  Can be yours
You'll have women that the whole
  World adores

SHE HOLDS OUT THE KEY, A CHARM SHE ONCE BOUGHT FROM
MOTHER HARE.

This charm will ever win you
  Fair girls to have and hold
Its power will continue
  When you grow old

None can refuse you
  You'll set their hearts on fire

They will always choose you
  When you so desire

I offer you perfection
  A love that will not die
Just for the selection
  Of my little pie.

> *PARIS* LOOKS INTERESTED. HE TAKES THE CHARM FROM *LOVEY*
> *MARS.* SHE DANCES OFF. *PARIS* PUTS THE CHARM IN HIS POCKET.
> THE THREE LADIES ENTER. AS THEY SING, THEY GROUP THEM-
> SELVES IN THE MANNER OF THE CLASSICAL PICTURES OF THE
> JUDGMENT OF PARIS.

THE THREE LADIES

Choose
Choose
What can you lose?
Award me the prize
And you'll never sing the blues.

> WITH ELABORATE POMP, *PARIS* AWARDS THE GOLDEN APPLE TO
> *LOVEY MARS.* THE OTHER TWO LADIES ARE INDIGNANT AS *LOVEY*
> AND *PARIS* DANCE OFF TO A RAUCOUS ONE-STEP.

MISS MINERVA *and* MRS. JUNIPER

It's a fraud!
It's a fraud!
The competition is a fraud

It's not he hasn't picked us
But Madam Mars has tricked us

Nice and sweet
We compete
But Lovey had to cheat

And she catered to his lechery
And won the prize by treachery

And fraud!
Fraud!

An awful fraud!
The judge is party to a fraud

The prize has been awarded
For motives much too sordid

To relate
Just you wait
They're trafficking with fate

What a mess there'll be
Wait and see

Lawd!
It's a fraud!

MISS MINERVA AND MRS. JUNIPER MARCH OFF. MEANWHILE THE
SCENE HAS CHANGED TO HELEN'S VERANDAH. HELEN SITS STAR-
ING AIMLESSLY AT THE MORNING GLORIES AROUND THE PICKET
FENCE, IDLY FANNING HERSELF. LOVEY MARS AND PARIS ENTER.

LOVEY MARS

Afternoon
Miz Helen

My it's awful hot
Isn't it?

HELEN

Uh huh.

SHE SEES *PARIS*.

Uuh *huh!*

LOVEY MARS

Mr. Paris
Meet Miz Helen
Lovely place she's got
Isn't it?

PARIS NODS QUIETLY. *HELEN* NODS BACK. THEY SMILE.

LOVEY MARS, *as* PARIS *softly dances*

Mister Paris is new in these parts, you see
    You've heard he's a traveling man
So give him a glass of nice ice tea
    And cool his brow with your fan.

HELEN

Uh huh.

LOVEY MARS

Thank you, Miz Helen

WITH A FAKE GESTURE OF SURPRISE, *LOVEY* CHATTERS TO THE
YOUNG COUPLE, WHO PAY NO ATTENTION TO HER AS THEY
MOVE TOWARD EACH OTHER.

Heavens it's so hot
I absolutely forgot

The Epworth League is due
To meet at half-past two

And I'm presiding
                    Oh dear! Oh dear!
I'll just have time to walk over
I'll leave Mister Paris here

You young folks must have lots to talk over.

                    HELEN, *dreamily*
Uh huh.

                    LOVEY MARS

Please excuse me, I'll have to fly
You'll find her *very* hospitable, Mr. Paris
Good-bye, my dears, good-bye.

        SHE WALTZES OFF.

        AS *PARIS* AND *HELEN* REACH OUT TOWARD EACH OTHER, THEY
        SUDDENLY BECOME AWARE THAT *ULYSSES* AND *THE BOYS* HAVE
        ENTERED ON THEIR WAY TO PLAY BALL. THEY ARE DRESSED IN
        CRUDE BASEBALL OUTFITS AND CARRY BATS AND GLOVE.

                    ACHILLES, AJAX *and* NESTOR
Afternoon
Miz Helen
                    ULYSSES, *mockingly*
My, it's awful hot
Isn't it?

PATROCLUS, DOC MACAHAN, DIOMEDE

Afternoon
Miz Helen

ULYSSES

My, it's *awful* hot
Isn't it?

AS THE BOYS SHAMBLE OFF, *PARIS* IMITATES THEM ANGRILY.
THEN, TIPPING HIS HAT TO *HELEN*, HE TURNS TO GO. *HELEN*
LEANS OVER THE PORCH RAIL AND GRABS HIM BY THE COLLAR.
HIS COAT COMES OFF EXHIBITING HIS TORSO DRESSED ONLY
IN A DICKEY, SUSPENDERS AND SHIRT CUFFS. SHE PULLS *PARIS*
DOWN BESIDE HER AND SERENADES HIM WITH A SUMMERY
WARMTH IN HER VOICE.

HELEN, *vocalizing languidly*

It's a lazy afternoon
  And the beetle bugs are zoomin
  And the tulip trees are bloomin
  And there's not another human
                In view
                But us two

It's a lazy afternoon
  And the farmer leaves his reapin
  In the meadows cows are sleepin
  And the speckled trout stop leapin
                Upstream
                As we dream

A fat pink cloud hangs over the hill
  Unfolding like a rose

If you hold my hand and sit real still
  You can hear the grass as it grows

It's a lazy afternoon
  And my rockin chair will fit yer
  And my cake was never richer
  And I've made a tasty pitcher
                Of tea
So spend this lazy afternoon with me

       SHE SEIZES *PARIS* BY THE HAIR AND TWIRLS HIM AROUND. HE
       LIES ON HIS STOMACH AS SHE LEANS AGAINST THE PORCH.

A fat pink cloud hangs over the hill
  Unfolding like a rose
If you hold my hand and sit real still
  You can hear the grass as it grows

It's a lazy afternoon
  And I know a place that's quiet
  Cept for daisies running riot
  And there's no one passing by it
              To see
Come spend this lazy afternoon with me.

       PARIS ELEGANTLY DANCES A PROPOSAL AND BRINGS DOWN HIS
       BALLOON WITH A FLICK OF HIS WRIST. *HELEN* FLINGS HERSELF
       INTO *PARIS'* ARMS.

               HELEN

All right, my dear, you talked me into it.

SHE KISSES HIM AND RUSHES INTO THE HOUSE. *PARIS*, BEWIL-
DERED, SEIZES A SUCCESSION OF CLOTHES AND PACKAGES AS
THEY FLY OUT OF THE WINDOW. *HELEN* APPEARS IN THE DOOR-
WAY, COMPLETELY DRESSED FOR TRAVEL IN A FLOATING LINEN
DUSTER AND A MOTORING HAT. SHE CARRIES A SMALL STATUE
OF *SEPTEMBER MORN*, A JEWEL CASKET AND A LARGE BOX LET-
TERED *CASH*. SHE GETS INTO THE BASKET OF THE BALLOON WITH
PARIS AND THEY BEGIN THEIR ASCENT.

MENELAUS SAUNTERS ON AT THIS MOMENT. HE LOOKS UP AND
IS FAINTLY NETTLED TO SEE HIS WIFE FLOATING IN THE AIR WITH
A STRANGER.

MENELAUS

Helen! Helen!
Oh you gave me a scare
What on earth are you doing up there?

LOVEY MARS RUSHES ON. *HELEN* HAPPILY WAVES GOOD-BYE TO
HER HUSBAND AS THE BALLOON DISAPPEARS.

LOVEY MARS, *aghast*

Helen! Paris!
You had better come back

MENELAUS RUNS INTO HIS HOUSE. HE KEEPS POPPING OUT TO
ITEMIZE HIS LOSSES.

MENELAUS

They took the china
And the bric a brac!

MISS MINERVA AND *MRS. JUNIPER*, THE BOYS IN THEIR BASEBALL
UNIFORMS, *ULYSSES* AND *PENELOPE* AND THE TOWNSPEOPLE
COME IN ONE AFTER THE OTHER.

LOVEY MARS

Helen! Paris!
You are liable to crash

MENELAUS, *in despair*

They also have the jewels
And the household cash!

LOVEY MARS

Paris! Helen!
You are trifling with fate!

MENELAUS

They also took the linen
And the silver plate!

MISS MINERVA *and* MRS. JUNIPER

Disgraceful!
  Unlawful!
Unwomanly!
  Perfidious!

See that brazen hussy
Crowing with delight!

MISS MINERVA, MRS. JUNIPER *and* WOMEN'S CHORUS

It's shocking!
  It's awful!
It's ghastly!
  It's hideous!

MOTHER HARE, *airily*

Good-bye, Helen
Don't forget to write.

TURNING, *MISS MINERVA AND MRS. JUNIPER SEE LOVEY MARS.*

MISS MINERVA

Ah ha! We knew it all along

MRS. JUNIPER

You knew he'd do it all along!
With tales of love you tricked him

MISS MINERVA

Now our Helen is the victim!

LOVEY MARS, *innocently*

You have no call to scold me so
He flattered and cajoled me so
I only introduced her
It was *Paris* who seduced her!

THE TOWNSPEOPLE

Helen, come back
Before it is too late!

MENELAUS, *wailing*

Bring back all the china
And the silver plate!

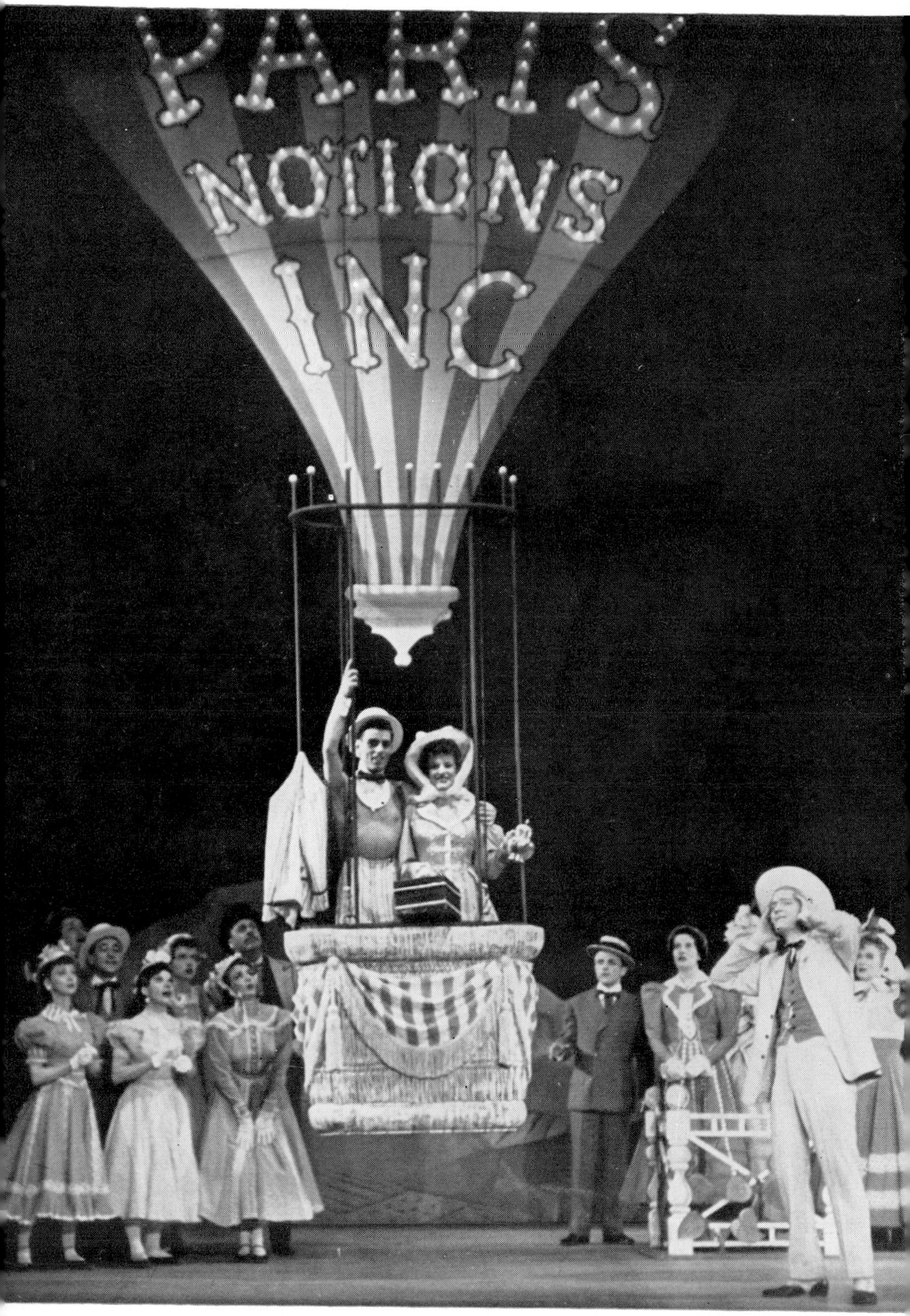
PARIS
NOTIONS
INC

THE TOWNSPEOPLE

Helen, come back
There's trouble piling up
Don't leave hearth and husband
For a worthless city pup!

**THE BOYS IN BLUE AND *ULYSSES* UNCONCERNEDLY TOSS A BALL
BACK AND FORTH. THEY INTERRUPT THEIR PRACTICE TO LOOK UP.**

THE BOYS, *casually*

Well well there goes Helen
Gone as the crow flies
                    Lost in the blue

Lucky Paris
Got our local heiress
Away goes Helen
                    Adieu, adieu!

MENELAUS, *outraged*

I can't believe my eyes
Are you carrying on as usual?
Paris hoodwinks us guys
Do such insults amuse you all?

THE BOYS

                    Play ball!
                    Play ball!

OLD MEN, *turning on them*

Have heroes grown so tame?
Does the pioneer blood run thin in you?
Haven't you any shame?
Is there no sense of sin in you?

ULYSSES

Paris is a shiftless cuss
And Helen is not much better

OLD MEN

To erase this blot
You boys have got
To storm the town and get her!
                    Get her!
                    Get Helen!

MENELAUS, *beseeching*

You swore upon your honor
You were hers to command
Now trouble is upon her
And you won't lift a hand

ULYSSES

The oath we made was sporting
It was peace we meant to bring
But aren't you guys distorting
The principle of the thing?

OLD MEN, *leaping at the phrase*

That's it! that's it!
It's the principle of the thing!
Get sore! Make war!
On wicked Rhododendron!

MENELAUS

We're too old to pull a trigger
We have seen too many winters
Were we young and full of vigor
We would tear that town to splinters

ULYSSES, *to his friends*

Pay no mind to all that pouting
Pay no mind to their disputing
Old men always do the shouting
Young men have to do the shooting

OLD MEN

But the principle, yes the principle
It's the principle of the thing
  Get out your guns
  And fix those sons
Of Rhododendron!

                 Vengeance

On Rhododendron!

                 Vengeance

On Rhododendron!

THE BOYS, *swayed*

Maybe they are right, Ulysses
Maybe we should go, Ulysses

OLD MEN, *pacing furiously*

Vengeance
Vengeance

THE BOYS

Maybe they are right, Ulysses
Maybe we should fight, Ulysses
Tell us yes or no, Ulysses

OLD MEN

Vengeance
Vengeance

MENELAUS

If we were your age
We would not permit
This sellout
We'd burn with rage
We'd champ the bit
And we would yell out

Vengeance!

THE BOYS

They're right! They're right!

MENELAUS

Of course we're right!

THE BOYS

Of course! Of course!

We can't stand by
And let that guy
Take our good Helen off by force!

It's vengeance! Vengeance! Vengeance!

THE OLD MEN CONTINUE TO CHANT VENGEANCE DURING THE FOLLOWING SECTION. THE BOYS IN BLUE JOIN THEM.

PENELOPE *and* THE THREE LADIES

Will you never learn?
When you return
The place for which you fought
May not be the same

No happiness is bought
With murder and flame
Only sorrow and shame
Only sorrow and shame

MENELAUS *and* THE BOYs

Ready, Ulysses?
Do you intend to go?

PENELOPE, *clinging to* ULYSSES

No, Ulysses
You promised me No.

THE THREE LADIES

Do not go, Ulysses
There is danger just ahead.

MOTHER HARE

Do not go, Ulysses
Stay home and die in bed.

**THEY ALL START SHOUTING AT HIM AT ONCE. WITH A SUDDEN
DECISION *ULYSSES* JOINS THE OLD MEN MARCHING ABOUT THE
STAGE. *MENELAUS* AND THE BOYS FALL IN BEHIND HIM.**

ULYSSES

Vengeance! Vengeance!

ALL THE MEN

Vengeance! Vengeance!

**AT A GESTURE FROM *ULYSSES*, THE BOYS IN BLUE RUN OFF STAGE
TO PREPARE FOR A DEPARTURE.**

ULYSSES, *to* PENELOPE

Oh nothing could be truer
Than the love I bear for you
  But duty to my fellow man
  Is greater than my private plan
And I must say adieu
And I must say adieu.

**HE EMBRACES HER FONDLY AND HURRIES OFF TO JOIN HIS
COMRADES.**

PENELOPE

Alas alas it's ever thus
The men talk love and beauty
  They kiss and vow and make a fuss
  But when they slip away from us
They blame it all on duty
They blame it all on duty.

ULYSSES AND HIS FRIENDS SLOWLY MOVE ON STAGE ENSCONCED
IN A FLOAT DRAPED WITH BUNTING. THE FLOAT HAS A PROUD
FIGUREHEAD WITH A MILITANT BUST AND A SILVER CROWN.
THE FIGUREHEAD TURNS TO THE EXCITED CROWD AND SINGS.

THE FIGUREHEAD

Row, boys, row
Row down the river
All ashore all ashore
That ain't coming with me

ULYSSES *and* THE BOYS

Whichaway
Whichaway
Does that old red river run?

THE MEN	*and*	THE WOMEN
From our back door		Remember what you promised
Down to the rising sun.		Do not go.

AT THE LAST MINUTE MENELAUS JUMPS ON THE FLOAT, WHICH
SAILS OFF WITH ULYSSES AND THE BOYS. ULYSSES STANDS AT
THE PROW. WATER RIPPLES OVER THE BACKDROP. THE OLD MEN
WAVE GOOD-BYE. PENELOPE AND THE WOMEN WEEP. MOTHER
HARE BITES HER THUMB AT THEM AS THE CURTAIN FALLS.

Act Two

ACT TWO

THE CURTAIN RISES ON THE BUSTLING CITY OF RHODODENDRON. SHOPS, FACTORIES, PARKS SUGGESTED. SMOKESTACKS ARE STILL RISING IN THE DISTANCE AS WE SEE THE MAIN STREET. *HELEN* IS TAKING THE AIR WITH *PARIS*. THEY ARE FOLLOWED BY A GROUP OF ELEGANT MEN ABOUT TOWN. *HELEN* IS SPLENDID IN AN OUTRAGEOUS GOWN, TWIRLING A LACY PARASOL. SHE IS HAVING A HIGH OLD TIME.

HELEN

Oh it's grand to see my picture in the papers
I adore a life that has a dash of spice
   My reputation's battered
   But it really hasn't mattered
Every lad about is mad about this bird of paradise!

Let the proper girls stay home and get the vapors
For me just put some bubbly on the ice
   My future may be stormy, dear
   But heavens, don't reform me, dear
I'm nicer as a nice girl who is really not too nice!

MEN ABOUT TOWN, *serenading her*

Oh it's grand to see her picture in the papers

HELEN, *in vaudeville style*

Looking ultra physical
And slightly aphrodisical

MEN

We adore a girl who has a dash of spice

HELEN

Mother may I go out to swim?
Where oh where is peeping Jim?

MEN

Her reputation's battered
But it seems it hasn't mattered
Every lad about is mad about that bird of paradise!

HELEN

Denounce me in the Capitol
But I don't care a rap at all

MEN

Let the proper girls stay home and get the vapors

HELEN, *doing a high kick*

You should really see me, dear
Swinging from a chandelier!

MEN

For her just put some bubbly on the ice

HELEN

Pol Roget and Veuve Cliquot
Swing your partner do si do

MEN

Her future may be stormy, dear

HELEN

But heavens, don't reform me, dear
I'm nicer as a nice girl who is really not too nice!

THE CITIZENS STRUT ON. THEY ARE FOLLOWED BY ULYSSES AND
HIS FRIENDS. HELEN IS HORRIFIED TO SEE THEM. AS SHE RECOILS,
AGHAST, THE BOYS AND THE TOWNFOLK ARE LEFT FACING EACH
OTHER LIKE TWO FOOTBALL TEAMS. MENELAUS MOURNFULLY
STANDS OFFSIDE.

ULYSSES

Helen, come back before it is too late!

MENELAUS, *whining*

Bring back all the china and the silver plate!

THE BOYS

Helen, come back
There's trouble piling up

Don't leave hearth and husband
For a worthless city pup

ULYSSES

Come home, Helen
All will be forgiven

MENELAUS

Come home, Helen
'Cause I miss you so

ULYSSES *and* THE BOYS

Come home, Helen
All will be forgotten!

HELEN

Thank you for the offer, boys
Thank you, but No.

ULYSSES AND THE BOYS TRY TO SEIZE HELEN. THE TOWNFOLK
INTERVENE. THERE IS A WILD SCRIMMAGE IN THE COURSE OF
WHICH HELEN AND THE TOWNFOLK ESCAPE. THE BOYS ARE LEFT
ALONE ON STAGE FACING THE SUDDENLY EMPTY STREET. HELEN'S
VOICE IS HEARD IN THE DISTANCE ECHOING EERILY.

HELEN, *off-stage*

Oh it's grand
To see my picture
In the papers

I adore a life
That has a dash
Of spice . . .

THE SKY DARKENS. THE BOYS LOOK DISCONSOLATE. ULYSSES
STUDIES THE TOWN WITH FASCINATION.

THE BOYS, *angrily*

Plumes on her hat and frivolous clothes
Laughs at us and thumbs her nose
We're a bunch of so and sos
   Let's go home! Let's go home!

ULYSSES, *calmly*

Helen is natcherly sinful
But the piper she'll have to pay
She's going to pay him in full
Cause we're taking her home today

THE BOYS

Bringing her home looked easy up there
But this town gives us a scare
Fellows, we ain't got a prayer
   Let's go home! Let's go home!

ULYSSES, *looking around*

See them buildings push the sky up
See them streets and railroads glisten
Never knew a town to fly up
So almighty fast as this 'n

THE BOYS

People like this we never could tame
City folks know every game
They can keep that dippy dame
   Let's go home! Let's go home!

ULYSSES

Don't give up so easy
Come back, you guys
Let's get in a huddle
And organize

THE BOYS

But they are so many
And we are so few
We will never break
This town in two.

ULYSSES

I figured out a simple trick
It's elementary arithmetic

They're bored and aimless
Their brains are blotto
Divide and conquer
Will be our motto

Watch me take the city
Watch me take the city
We'll take over their community

THE BOYS, *inspired*

Just give us the opportunity!

ULYSSES

Paint some placards
And phone the scare sheets
Write some torrid
Horrid tearsheets

Get some pamphlets
To the printers
And we will knock the town to splinters!

HIS HENCHMEN RUN OFF TO PREPARE THE CAMPAIGN. SOME
BUSY CITIZENS OF RHODODENDRON SCURRY PAST.

ULYSSES, *stopping them*

Hey you

CITIZENS

Hey who?

ULYSSES

You and *you.*
Let's form a committee.

CITIZENS

Form a committee?
Committee for what?

ULYSSES, *intensely*

Don't ask questions
Are you joining or not?
All you have to do is sign
Right here on the dotted line.

CITIZENS, *signing*

Mutter mutter
And grumble grumble

ULYSSES

Now you're a committee.

CITIZENS, *forming a group*
Mutter mutter
And grumble grumble.

ANOTHER GROUP OF CITIZENS ENTER. ULYSSES HAILS THEM AND
POINTS TO THE FIRST GROUP.

ULYSSES

Ladies and gents
Start getting wise
It's time that you opened up your eyes

Your city is proud
It's strong and it's tall
But *they* are out to ruin it all

THE SECOND GROUP

Heavens, what a horrid crew!
What on earth are we to do?

ULYSSES

As your spokesman
I deplore em
Line up here and make a quorum

All join hands
And look real pretty
And we will form a counter committee!

BOTH GROUPS

Mutter mutter
And grumble grumble

ULYSSES AND THE SIX SINGING BOYS GO INTO A HUDDLE. HE
COACHES THEM ON THEIR NEXT MOVE.

ULYSSES

Now we'll take the city.

BOTH GROUPS

Mutter mutter
And grumble grumble

PATROCLUS, ACHILLES AND NESTOR JOIN THE FIRST GROUP. THE
OTHER THREE JOIN THE SECOND GROUP. THEY LEAD THE CITI-
ZENS AS THEY ANGRILY CHANT.

FIRST GROUP	SECOND GROUP
Give up Helen	Don't ditch Helen
She's a public scandal	You're a rat unless you're
Send back Helen	Loyal to Helen
She's too hot to handle	Don't give in to pressure
Send back Helen	Save our Helen
Give that baby doll up	Listen here to this you
Get rid of Helen	Raise hell for Helen
Helen is a trollop	She's a civic issue

OTHERS OF ULYSSES' FRIENDS APPEAR WITH PLACARDS, POSTERS
AND LEAFLETS. THE TWO GROUPS GROW MORE BELLICOSE.

Send back Helen   Save our Helen

Give up Helen   Don't ditch Helen
Get rid of Helen   Raise hell for Helen

Get rid of Helen   Save our Helen
Get rid of Helen   Save our Helen

PANDEMONIUM BREAKS OUT. THEY BEGIN FIGHTING WILDLY.
HECTOR, THE MAYOR OF RHODODENDRON, COMES FORWARD,
HOLDING UP HIS HANDS. *MAYOR HECTOR* IS THE ESSENCE OF THE
BIG CITY ITSELF. A SPRY, DAPPER GENTLEMAN WHOSE CORRUP-
TION IS MASKED BY A CROCODILE SMILE AND AN OCCASIONAL
CROCODILE TEAR. HE IS INEVITABLY HIGHHATTED, SPATTED,
MORNINGCOATED AND STRIPEDTROUSERED. HIS KEYNOTE IS
CHEERY ELEGANCE AND HIS BLAND TACTICS ARE WINNING AND
LETHAL. HE MOVES THROUGH THE ALIENATED CROWD OF CITI-
ZENS AND BLITHELY PRESENTS HIMSELF TO *ULYSSES*.

HECTOR

I'm Mayor Hector. Here is my card
I'm happy to meet you guys
Maybe you're taking this too hard
Why don't we compromise?

Why break the town up? Nothing is solved
I have a practical plan
Let's have the two galoots involved
Fight it out man to man!

ULYSSES, *mollified*

That's fair and square! A practical plan.

THE BOYS, *joining in*

Let's settle the issue man to man.

ULYSSES

And Mayor Hector will be
The referee

THE BOYS *and* THE CITIZENS

We agree!

A SPACE CLEARS QUICKLY AS A ROPE IS BROUGHT OUT AND IS
HELD BY THE CROWD TO INDICATE A PRIZE-FIGHT RING. A STREET
LAMP IS BENT OVER THE CENTER AREA. AT A SIGNAL FROM
HECTOR IT LIGHTS UP AND TRANSFORMS THE STREET INTO A
PRIZE-FIGHT ARENA. *ULYSSES* DRAGS FORTH THE RELUCTANT
MENELAUS AND GIVES HIM A QUICK BRUSH-UP COURSE IN THE
GENTLE ART OF FISTICUFFS.

ULYSSES, *shadowboxing*

Lead with the left
Block with the right
Move in close
And hold in the clinches
Jab and duck
Cross with your right

MENELAUS TRIES VAINLY TO EMULATE *ULYSSES* BUT STEPS IN TOO
CLOSE AND IS ACCIDENTALLY KNOCKED OUT. *PARIS* ENTERS THE
RING IN A BRIGHT SILK ROBE WITH *PARIS* EMBLAZONED ON
THE BACK.

THE BOYS

Look out!

THE EAGER BOYS PUSH *ULYSSES* INTO THE RING. *PARIS* IS STAR-
TLED TO SEE THAT HIS OPPONENT IS NOT THE FRAIL *MENELAUS*
BUT THE MORE IMPOSING *ULYSSES*. AFTER A NERVOUS RECOIL
HE BEGINS TO DANCE ABOUT IN THE MANNER OF THE OLD
PUGILISTS.

THE BOYS

Take him on, Ulysses
Attaboy, Ulysses!

THE CROWD GREETS *PARIS* WITH A ROAR OF APPROVAL WHICH
THEN GROWS INTO A STEADY MASS OF SOUND AND CONTINUES
THROUGHOUT THE PRIZE FIGHT.

ALTHOUGH CHOREOGRAPHED IN THE PERIOD MANNER, THE PRIZE
FIGHT SHOULD NOT BE PRECIOUS IN STYLE. IT SHOULD CONVEY,
FOR INSTANCE, THE VITALITY OF BELLOWS' *THE KNOCK OUT AT
SMOKY JOE'S*. THE CROWD REACTS TO THE ACTION WITH GRUNTS,
YELLS, SCREAMS, HISSES, BOOS, CATCALLS AND GROANS.

DURING THE FIGHT THE BOYS ARE VERY BUSY ALTERNATELY
CHEERING *ULYSSES* AND MAKING BETS ON THE OUTCOME.
HECTOR, DURING THE CLINCHES, TRIES TO RABBIT PUNCH *ULYSSES*
ON THE SLY.

ULYSSES FINALLY CONNECTS WITH *PARIS'* CHIN AND KNOCKS
HIM OUT. THE BOYS ARE JUBILANT AS *HECTOR* RAISES *ULYSSES'*
ARM IN THE TRADITIONAL SIGNIFICATION OF THE WINNER. BUT
THE CROWD GROANS AS *ULYSSES* KNOCKS OUT *PARIS* AND THE
SHOUTING FADES AWAY INTO SILENCE.

PARIS IS SADLY CARRIED AWAY BY THE TOWNFOLK IN A CORTEGE
REMINISCENT OF THE DEATH EXIT IN *HAMLET*. AS THEY LEAVE,

THE TOWNFOLK PAY OFF THEIR BETS WITH THE BOYS, WHO ARE
LEFT WITH FISTFULS OF BILLS.

ULYSSES AND HIS BAND ARE ALONE ON STAGE AS HECTOR
COMES FORWARD LEADING HELEN BY THE HAND. THE BOYS EYE
HER SCORNFULLY AS THEY POCKET THEIR WINNINGS. HELEN
TRIES TO CARRY OFF THE SITUATION WITH BRAVADO, BUT IT IS
NOT EASY. SHE WAVES TO MENELAUS AND POUTS WHEN HE
LOOKS SEVERELY AT HER.

MENELAUS

After all you've been to me
How could you treat me so, my lamb?

HELEN

I can't think what got into me
You know how helpless I am.

On champagne and quail
They wined, dined and supped me
They knew I was frail
They tried to corrupt me!

MENELAUS, *melting completely*

Let's go home.

HELEN

Uh huh.

BOTH

Let's go home.

AS THEY EXIT HELEN LOOKS BACK AT THE BOYS, SHRUGS AND
STICKS OUT HER TONGUE.

THE BOYS, *despairing*

After keeping us all on needles and pins
And reducing the town to shambles
She winks her eye, her old man grins
And back to home she ambles

Is there no justice?
Does virtue never triumph?
The wicked like a bay tree
Keep right on flourishing.

ULYSSES

She'll pay for her crime
In the Lord Almighty's time
It wasn't her we fought for
'Twas the principle of the thing.

HECTOR

Please pardon my distress if I
Upset a phrase you love
But would you kindly specify
The *thing* it was the *principle* of?

THE BOYS

The principle, hmmmmm
                    The principle, well
The reason that we begun it

ULYSSES

The important thing isn't the principle
The important thing is *we won it.*

THE BOYS, *slightly doleful*

We certainly did. We won it.

NIGHT DESCENDS ON RHODODENDRON. THE LIGHTS GLOW IN
THE DISTANCE. A DISTURBING ATMOSPHERE.

ULYSSES, *cheerily*

Before we head back for the hills
We owe ourselves a treat
  It's Saturday night
  The lights are bright
And we're on Easy Street

THE BOYS

We've got money in our jeans
Let's dress up and look really pretty

ULYSSES

  Come along boys
  Let's make some noise
And see what's what in the great big city.

THE SHOP WINDOWS LIGHT UP. THE SKYLINE GLITTERS.

HECTOR, *stepping from a shadow*

Step in a while
At the mercantile store

And you'll come out looking
Like you never did before

In store-bought suits
You raw recruits
Will look as chic
As the sleekest city dude

> ULYSSES AND THE BOYS GO INTO THE MERCANTILE STORE. HEC-
> TOR STEPS FORWARD AND ADDRESSES THE AUDIENCE DIRECTLY.
> HERE, AS ALWAYS, HECTOR PERFORMS IN A MAMMY-SINGER STYLE
> REPLETE WITH NASAL TREMOLO AND THROBBING SENTIMENTAL-
> ITY. THE TOTAL EFFECT SHOULD BE ONE OF SUGARY INNOCENCE
> WHICH UNDERLIES THE EMPTY CYNICISM OF HIS SONG.

HECTOR

Now we will have our revenge on them
The bait is ready, the trap is set
The city itself will be our stratagem
There'll be a bitter reckoning yet

They speak of seven sins in the Scripture
But our age has invented many more
So subtle and sweet that once you've slipped you're
Never never able to go home any more

> HE TWIRLS HIS CANE JAUNTILY AND EXECUTES A FEW SOFT-SHOE
> TURNS.

Some can be bought for money
And some there are that glory can buy
  Some yield their purity

In search of security
And some drown their dreams in a bottle of rye

Some go for empty knowledge
And some think sex will set their body free
   The man of the hour
   Will settle for power
Yes, every soul alive has his fee

     Except for noble people
     Like you and like me
     With the exception
     Of you and me

Now is the time to take them. Nightfall
The city waits, half awake half asleep
Its many eyes watch, its many voices call
Its many hands reach out, the shadows are deep

The seven sins will rise up to tempt these men
And see they never never go home again
Now let the city find which ones are easy game
For the tricky little pitfall of fame

Some can be bought for money
And some there are that glory can buy
   Some yield their purity
   In search of security
And some drown their dreams in a bottle of rye

Some go for empty knowledge
And some think sex will set their body free

The man of the hour
Will settle for power
Yes, every soul alive has his fee

    Except for noble people
      lovely people
      wonderful people
      marvelous people
      exceptional people
        like you
        and
        like me!

HE EXITS WITH A VAUDEVILLE STRUT.

THE CURTAINS PART TO REVEAL *ULYSSES'* HOUSE IN ANGEL'S
ROOST. *PENELOPE* SITS IN A VINE-COVERED GAZEBO, BUSILY
AT WORK ON A SECTION OF PATCHWORK QUILT. A COUPLE OF
SUITORS ARE MOONING ABOUT. THEY HOLD OUT NOSEGAYS
TO HER. SHE SHOOS THEM AWAY A COUPLE OF TIMES AND THEY
RELUCTANTLY LEAVE.

HELEN ENTERS, LEANING AFFECTIONATELY ON THE ARM OF
MENELAUS. SHE IS WEARING HER TRAVELING DUSTER AND
MOTORING VEIL AND CARRIES THE CASH BOX IN HER ARM AS
A TOKEN OF HER NEW MARITAL STABILITY. *PENELOPE* LOOKS UP
FROM HER WORK AND SMILES AT THEM.

HELEN, *in a hot blues tempo*

Well tell the folks I'm back again
From that horrid torrid town
My trolley's on the track again
I'm settling down

MENELAUS

She is a good girl
A good girl
A little misunderstood girl
But she's gonna settle down

HELEN

Uh huh
Now I'm gonna settle down.

From now on married bliss is
Good enough for me.

PENELOPE, *anxiously*

But what about Ulysses?

HELEN

He is off on a spree

MENELAUS

He and the fellers
Those fellers
Are rowdy dowdy hellers

HELEN

I was shocked as I could be
Uh huh
Just as shocked as I could be

PENELOPE

The shape of the world is round
Is round

And no matter how far he'll stray
When the thread of his dream's unwound
He's bound
To turn up at his own back door one day

HELEN

Penelope, you're a good girl
But your good man likes to roam
Why can't a good woman
Ever keep a good man home?

When you're too proper
With poppa
You're sure to come a cropper

Cause they never will stay home
Uh *huh*
You can never keep them home.

HELEN SMILES AT HER A TRIFLE GLOATINGLY AND SASHAYS OUT.
MENELAUS PAUSES A MOMENT, PLACING A QUIET HAND ON
PENELOPE'S SHOULDER. SHE HAS RESUMED WORK ON THE PATCH-
WORK PIECES.

PENELOPE

I'll just keep busy
Till good fortune
Brings him back in view

MENELAUS

But won't you be lonely, Penelope
Aren't you worried wondering

What he may be up to wandering
Away from you?

After all, Ulysses
May be gone for quite a spell
What if he finds that you
Have changed as well?

We don't get any younger
Everything ages but the heart's hunger.

MENELAUS WANDERS OFF.

PENELOPE, *tenderly*

He brought me windflowers that grow among the rocks
And picked me wild berries bitter to the tongue
He taught me to tell time by the dandelion clocks
When we were young
            When we were young

He caught me a mockingbird and wove a willow cage
A cage from the willow where we kissed and clung
He fought me fierce dragons. We were princess and a page
When we were young
            When we were young

Then we stood up in church
And we whispered vows
And he took me to a mountain peak
And built me a house

The berries and the flowers and the dandelions fade
The songbird is silent, shivering in the cold

The dragons come creeping and they tell me I'm afraid
That I'll grow old
                        That I'll grow old

And I lie in the house
As the stars grow dim
And I think of how his body was
So warm, warm and slim

And I know there ain't no growing old
For me and for him.
No, never, never
Not for me and him.

**THE LIGHTS FADE ON *PENELOPE* AND COME UP ON THE TOWN
OF RHODODENDRON.**

THE BIG SPREE

ULYSSES' WANDERING BEGINS. THE ACTION SHIFTS TO A RE-
VIEW STYLE. THE PROSCENIUM BRIGHTENS WITH A FRAME OF
GLOWING LIGHTS. THE ARCH AND THE BACKDROP ARE BLACK,
AGAINST WHICH EACH SUCCESSIVE SET FLOATS ON AND OFF
WITH THE DECEPTIVE INTENSITY OF ILLUSIONS.

EACH NUMBER IS PERFORMED IN THE SONG STYLE INDICATED
IN THE DIRECTION, BUT THE PERFORMER SHOULD ATTEMPT TO
HEIGHTEN THIS STYLE SO THAT AN AWARENESS OF TIME PASS-
ING IS COMMUNICATED TO THE AUDIENCE.

IN FRONT OF A SOLID VELOUR DROP, *ULYSSES* STRUTS ON, DAZ-
ZLING IN A BLACK SUIT WITH RED PIPING, A STRAW HAT AND
SPATS.

ULYSSES

I've got a store-bought suit
With a fancy plaid
It's a wonderful sight to see

I've got a store-bought suit
With a fancy plaid
And it fits just like a glove on me
  Fits just like a glove on me

I've got a store-bought suit
It's the first I've had
I've been waiting a long long time

I've got a store-bought suit
It's the first I've had
And now I'm right
                    In the height
                              Of style
I'm right in the height of style

THE SIX SINGING BOYS ENTER, ALSO CLAD IN BLACK WITH
VARIED PIPING.

Silver buttons and a checkered vest
Belted back and peaked lapels
When I swell my manly chest
Watch me wow them city belles!

'Cause in a store-bought suit
I'm a proud galoot
And the fruit
  Of the loom is mine

I was a raw recruit
But in a store-bought suit
I won't wither on the vine
Just you watch me
                    Rise and shine

THE BOYS PROUDLY SHOW OFF THEIR NEW CLOTHES.

ULYSSES *and* THE BOYS

Dressed in a store-bought suit
With a fancy stripe
I'm a rube
      On a jubilee

I was a raw recruit
But the time is ripe
For a wing ding of a jamboree
  Let's go on a great big spree!

ULYSSES

I'm a gay dog out to learn new tricks
And I'll follow every lead
I'm a slow poke from the sticks
But from now on watch my speed

ULYSSES *and* THE BOYS

'Cause in a store-bought suit
I'm a proud galoot
And it's Saturday night I see

So let the trumpets toot
I am out to hoot
And I'm ready for a Big Spree
A knock down
          drag out
              Spree!

HECTOR APPEARS OUT OF THE SHADOWS, A MOCKING SMILE ON HIS FACE. HE PASSES AROUND A FLASK. THE BOYS DRINK EAGERLY. *PARIS* APPEARS AND, AT A WINK FROM *HECTOR*, DISAPPEARS TO PRODUCE THE FIRST TEMPTATION OF THE BIG CITY. *HECTOR* BEGINS A BARKER SPIEL.

HECTOR

Hurryhurry
Right this way
For Rho
      do
           dendron
On display
The Wonder of the Twentieth Century
Here's
     Money
         Power
             Booze
And wenchery

Hurryhurry
Come with me
Get
  set
    for
The Big Spree!

(FROM NOW ON ALL THE PEOPLE *ULYSSES* WILL MEET ARE PLAYED BY CHARACTERS FROM HIS HOME TOWN. HE DOES NOT RECOGNIZE THEM, BUT THERE IS A HIDDEN REACTION IN HIM EACH TIME ONE OF THESE HOME FOLKS APPEARS. HIS EXCITEMENT FOR THE UNKNOWN GRADUALLY DWINDLES AS THE FAMILIAR FACES REAPPEAR, STRANGELY TRANSFORMED IN THE CITY NIGHT.)

BUT THE SPREE IS JUST BEGINNING AND HE IS READY FOR ANY-
THING AS *MADAME CALYPSO* RUSHES TO MEET HIM, LED ON BY
A SMIRKING *PARIS. CALYPSO* IS PLAYED BY *MRS. JUNIPER,* THE
SOCIAL ARBITER OF ANGEL'S ROOST. THIS CITY EQUIVALENT,
HOWEVER, IS A STATELY CREATURE IN AN EXTRAVAGANT BALL
GOWN. HER HAIR IS A WILDERNESS OF OSPREY PLUMES AND
HER EARS AND THROAT ARE ABLAZE WITH DIAMONDS. SHE
CARRIES AN ENORMOUS FAN WHICH SHE WAVES ALOFT AS SHE
SAILS MAJESTICALLY ACROSS THE STAGE.

CALYPSO

Ulysses Ulysses
At last, my dear
I've tracked you down
I've been combing every street in town
　You don't know *me*
　But I know *you*
And the *rest* of you darlings too

HECTOR, *presenting her*

Haven't you heard
Of Madame Calypso?
The nympho megalo ego dipso
Maniac who sets the pace in
Rhododendron? You've seen her face in
The social columns and front page scandals
Oh, she's the hostess who only handles
Big Names (both the Best and Worst Names)
Call celebrities by their first names.

CALYPSO

Ulysses and Doc
Achilles and *all*
You mustn't be late to the Victory Ball

ULYSSES

All of us
Would be delighted
Only we were
Never invited

CALYPSO

Darling
The ball's in honor of you
And all the rest
Of your brawny crew!

CALYPSO WAVES HER HAND. THE CURTAINS OPEN. A BLAZING
CHANDELIER AND BRIGHT YELLOW COLUMNS FLY INTO VIEW. A
HUGE YELLOW POUF ROLLS ON. THROUGH TWO ARCHWAYS A
CROWD OF GORGEOUSLY ATTIRED LADIES AND GENTLEMEN IN
WHITE TIE RUSH TO MEET THE BOYS DURING THE FOLLOWING
SECTION. THE BOYS, WHO HAVEN'T MOVED, ARE DELIGHTFULLY
BEWILDERED BY THE WONDERS OF THIS SALON THAT HAS FORMED
AROUND THEM.

CALYPSO

Spare no expense!

The best of everything

Tonight the welkin

Is going to ring

The champagne's iced

The bunting is swagged

And everyone's coming at ten!
To meet the brace
                    Of lions I've bagged
For my million-dollar den!

THE GUESTS BEGIN TO FAWN UNASHAMEDLY ON THE BASHFUL
MOUNTAIN BOYS.

WOMEN

Aren't they beauts?
Adorable brutes
So primitive, dashing and new

MEN, *to* CALYPSO

To think that our crowd is
Mixing with rowdies
Who would have dared it but you?

CALYPSO

The Old Guard is dying to stop me
Because I am up to the minute
The Social Register surely would drop me
Except
I've never been in it!

ULYSSES

Let them lift up a lorgnette
And eye you with scorn, yet
Beneath your fuss and feathers
I see a simple nymph.

CALYPSO, *coyly*

Just a shy nymph who caters
To good-looking satyrs
If passion I've perfected
That's expected of a nymph

A MALE GUEST

Who has money and lands
And remarkable glands
With an extra supply of lymph!

ALL THE GUESTS

She's a shy nymph who caters
To good-looking satyrs
If passion she's perfected
That's expected of a nymph.

CALYPSO AND HER GUESTS RECEIVE GLASSES OF CHAMPAGNE
AND LIFT THEM AS THEY TOAST ULYSSES AND HIS FRIENDS.

CALYPSO

Here's to you darlings from the hills

MEN *and* WOMEN

Marvelous
Simply marvelous!

CALYPSO

Thirteen uncouth youthful thrills!

MEN *and* WOMEN

Marvelous
Simply marvelous!

ULYSSES, *to the boys*

These folks aren't mad we won our campaign
They want to toast us all with champagne
But we're just plain dirt farmers, ma'am
No one for fine folk to salaam.

CALYPSO

Dear Milton was a farmer too
My late lamented husband Milton
A simple farmer just like you
With big broad shoulders I could wilt on

But
Milton struck it rich!
He peeled a hazel switch

He called it a divining rod
A simply *too* divining rod
That showed him soil
Just *soaked* in oil
It rushed
          And gushed
                    And made a wad
And now he's dead
And under the sod
But Milton struck it rich, thank God
Milton struck it rich

But you and your crew
Are excitingly new
You're the public's idols
And that is why, dolls
We're all in your power
You're the men of the hour
So we wine and dine you
And underline you.

ULYSSES AND THE BOYS ARE QUITE DELIGHTED WITH THE PRAISE
AND BURSTING WITH PRIDE. THEY STRUT ABOUT FOR THE CROWD.

ULYSSES *and* THE BOYS

'Cause we have a knack
We're the tip of the top
The pick of the pack
And the cream of the crop
We're thrilling
And marvelous
New and terrific
The boast
Of the coast
That is called the Pacific
Wonderful
Wonderful
Wonderful
Wonderful *us!*

AS THE BOYS DANCE IN A DREAM OF GLORY, SUDDENLY CALYPSO
AND HER GUESTS LOSE INTEREST IN THEM. CALYPSO YAWNS.

CALYPSO

Whatever became of Ulysses
Clever, clever Ulysses?
Whatever became of Ulysses
And all of his wonderful crew?

ULYSSES *and* THE BOYS

Why, here we are Madame Calypso
See us, Madame Calypso?
Remember us, Madame Calypso?

CALYPSO

Ye-es
Whatever became of you?

CALYPSO MOVES AWAY FROM ULYSSES AND THE ASTONISHED
BOYS. HER GUESTS FOLLOW HER. PATROCLUS TRIES TO DETAIN
HER AS SHE SAILS TOWARD THE EXIT. THE OTHER GUESTS FADE
IMPERCEPTIBLY. PATROCLUS, RELUCTANT TO LOSE THIS TASTE OF
GLORY, DESERTS HIS FRIENDS AND FOLLOWS HER.

PATROCLUS, *frantically*

I know a few tricks
To wow the grandstands
Bright, funny new tricks
I can do handstands!

I know some hard tricks
That will surprise folks
I can do card tricks!
I hypnotize folks.

HE AND *CALYPSO* DISAPPEAR WITH THE SUDDENNESS OF A
MAGIC TRICK.

ULYSSES

Patroclus!

THERE IS NO ANSWER. THE SET FLIES OFF SWIFTLY INTO SPACE,
LEAVING A VAST DARKNESS. THE BOYS STARE UP, OPEN-
MOUTHED.

ULYSSES, *with a shrug*

The cage is gone
The bird has flown

THE BOYS

Let him get home on his own.

HECTOR COMES FORWARD OUT OF THE SHADOWS.

ULYSSES

How many miles to Paradise Alley?

HECTOR

Three score and ten.

ULYSSES

Can we get there by morning light?

HECTOR

Yes.
And back again.

UI YSSES

Let's go on down to Paradise Alley
Where all the fields are green

THE BOYS

Let's go on down to Paradise Alley
And see what's to be seen.

A DROLL FIGURE ON ONE ROLLER SKATE CHARGES ON. A SIGN
SEWED TO HIS BACK PROCLAIMS *RUNNER*. HE WHISPERS WITH
HECTOR, NODS AND ROLLS OFF ON ONE FOOT LIKE A MERCURY
IN FLIGHT.

HECTOR TAKES OUT A HIP FLASK WHICH HE PASSES TO *ULYSSES*
AND THE BOYS. THEY TAKE LONG SWALLOWS.

HECTOR

Want to be an empire builder?
Want to play the game of games?
Drachma
        dollar
                ducat
                        guilder
One big fact with different names.

THE CURTAIN FLIES UP TO REVEAL AN ABSTRACTION OF A STOCK-
EXCHANGE FLOOR. A FUNCTIONAL WALNUT-TONED COUNTER
EXTENDS ACROSS THE REAR OF THE STAGE. EIGHT MALE CHORIS-
TERS, SOMEHOW SUGGESTING BULLS AND BEARS, SURGE AROUND
THE COUNTER.

HECTOR

Step into these stately portals
Where the Golden Calf is fed.
Shun the humbler working materials
Let them work for you instead.

UNDER *HECTOR'S* GUIDANCE, THE BOYS AND *ULYSSES* GO BACK
TO THE GROUP. *HECTOR* LEAPS UP ONTO THE COUNTER AS
SCYLLA ENTERS AND ALSO LEAPS ONTO THE COUNTER. MR.
SCYLLA IS *MENELAUS.* HE IS DRESSED IN AN EXTRAVAGANTLY
VAUDEVILLE VERSION OF WHAT THE WELL-DRESSED STOCK BROKER
WEARS. HE IS RAUCOUSLY JOLLY AND THE MELODY ECHOES THIS
MOOD.

SCYLLA

Oh Mister Charybdis

HECTOR

Oh yes, Mr Scylla?

SCYLLA

How's that brand new yacht you got?

HECTOR

How goes your villa?

SCYLLA

Oh the upkeep keeps me down
So I'm moving back to town

HECTOR

And his wife is wearing last year's old chinchilla.

SCYLLA

I say there, Charybdis

HECTOR

Oh yes, good friend Scylla?

SCYLLA

Did you corner the hemp market in Manila?

HECTOR

I did corner it, old sport
But I had to sell it short

SCYLLA

Positively, Mister Charybdis?

HECTOR

Absolutely, Mister Scylla.

MR. *SCYLLA* COMES DOWN OFF THE COUNTER AND GOES OVER
TO THE BOYS. *HECTOR* (CHARYBDIS) REMAINS ON THE COUNTER
ATTENDING TO THE BUYING AND SELLING.

SCYLLA

He pretends he sold hemp short
So as not to let the rest in
If you are the clever sort
Hemp's the thing you will invest in.

THE CROWD

Hurry
Hurry

Buy it
Sell it
Hurry
Buy it
Sell it
Now!

THE BOYS

We would like to buy some shares
But we lack the dough to cash in

AJAX

If we pool our railroad fares
And those bets we won we'll cash in!

THE CROWD

Hurry
Hurry
Buy it
Sell it
Hurry
Buy it
Sell it
Now!

ULYSSES *and* THE BOYS, *making a rowing gesture*

If we lose our railroad fares
Gettin home will be a nuisance

AJAX

If we win we're millionaires
By investing just a few cents!

THE CROWD

Hurry
Hurry
Buy it
Sell it
Hurry
Buy it
Sell it
Now!

AJAX SNATCHES THEIR MONEY FROM THEM AND RUNS UP TO
THE COUNTER. HE COMES BACK WITH A FISTFUL OF SHARES.

ULYSSES *and* THE BOYS

One-quarter
Half
Three-quarters
      Wow!
We think you ought
To sell it now!

AJAX

Rising hemp will turn the trick
And here is where we get rich quick!

SCYLLA JUMPS BACK UP ON THE COUNTER AND HE AND *HECTOR*
GO BACK INTO THEIR ROUTINE.

SCYLLA

Oh Mister Charybdis

HECTOR

Oh yes, Mister Scylla?

SCYLLA

How'd your big-game hunting go?

HECTOR

Got one gorilla.

SCYLLA

Bought a vineyard up in Maine
That makes passable champagne

HECTOR

Though his ulcers keep him down to sarsparilla

SCYLLA

Excuse me, Charybdis

HECTOR

Oh yes, good friend Scylla?

SCYLLA

Speaking of Manila hemp

HECTOR

You mean vanilla?
I just swept the market clean
Of that sweet vanilla bean

SCYLLA

Hemp's a bust then, Mr. Charybdis?

HECTOR

It's a wash out, Mr. Scylla!

MR. SCYLLA SMILES, SHRUGS, POPS A CIGAR IN AJAX'S MOUTH
AND TROTS OFF. THE CROWD VANISHES. AJAX CLAPS HIS HAND
OVER HIS FOREHEAD IN DESPAIR. HECTOR INDICATES THE WIN-
DOW WITH A GALLANT GESTURE. AJAX TAKES A RUNNING JUMP
AND CRASHES THROUGH IT. HECTOR DISCREETLY PULLS DOWN
THE SHADE AS THE BOYS RUSH FORWARD. HE PLACES HIS HAT
OVER HIS HEART AND LOWERS HIS EYES.

ULYSSES *and* THE BOYS

Poor Ajax!

THE STOCK EXCHANGE FADES. HECTOR AGAIN PASSES HIS FLASK
AROUND. CAPT. MARS GETS ILL AND STAGGERS OFF, BUT NO
ONE NOTICES.

HECTOR, *consolingly*

Does the way that things are going upset you?
Does the rattle of the city seem to get you?
Are your nerves a trifle edgy?
Has your brain begun to vegetate?
Is your love life in a hassle?
Has your mind begun to vacillate?
Would you care for a carefree diversion?
Leave this sordid little place for a while?
Won't you join me on a Saturday excursion
To our lovely desert isle?

ULYSSES, *to the boys*

What say?

THE BOYS

Okay.

ULYSSES, *cheerful again*

Then let's get under way.

THE CURTAIN RISES ON A GARISH WATER-FRONT DIVE BACKED
BY A DROP COMPLETE WITH VOLCANO AND CLOUD-HAUNTED
TROPICAL MOON. *THE SIREN* (PLAYED BY *LOVEY MARS*) WEARS
A BLACK WIG AND IS SWATHED IN LEIS. SHE SITS ON A PLAT-
FORM PULLED IN BY FOUR SIRENETTES. THE PLATFORM IS A
CLUMP OF FLOWERS TERMINATING IN A LIVID PALM TREE.

THE SIREN

By a goona goona goona
By a goona goona goona lagoon
We will croona croona croona
We will croona croona real jungle tune.

Upon that golden shore, kids,
We'll lie on beds of orchids
And then later
                    By the crater
                              Of the old volcano
We can promise we won't say No
A Noa

Let's a goa
Let's a go a go a go away soon
Where breezes blow a
Blow a blow a
Breezes blow a like a big big bassoon

Snug as two baboons
In a bamboo tree
I'll bamboozle you
And you'll bamboozle me
By a goona goona goona
By a goona goona goona lagoon.

SIX DANCING SIRENETTES HULA ON.

SIRENETTES

Woo   Woo   Woo
Woo oo   Woo oo   Woo oo

DESPITE *ULYSSES'* WARNING GESTURE THE BOYS HAVE GOTTEN
INTO THE SPIRIT OF IT ALL. THEY LUSTILY JOIN IN THE SINGING
AND DANCING. *ULYSSES* FINDS HIMSELF THE OBJECT OF *THE
SIREN'S* ATTENTIONS. HE BEGINS TO DISPLAY A TRACE OF PAGAN
ABANDON IN SPITE OF HIMSELF.

THE BOYS *and* THE SIRENETTES

Woo   Woo   Woo
Woo oo   Woo oo   Woo oo

ALL

By a goona goona goona
By a goona goona goona lagoon
We will spoona spoona spoona
We will spoona spoona beneath the moon.

THE BOYS

Those hula dancing mamas
Are really yama yamas

ULYSSES

They can shake and they can shimmy
Till they charm wild cobras

THE SIREN

Also fellas, they wear no bras!

ULYSSES *and* THE BOYS

Aloha loha loha

SIRENETTES

Let's a go a go a go away soon

THE BOYS

We will throw a throw a throw a
We will throw a throw a big big harpoon

ULYSSES

We'll hunt and fish a the whole day long

THE SIREN

Whatever you wish a just sound the gong

ALL

By that goona goona goona
By that goona goona goona lagoona lagoona lagoon

THE SIREN

The passion fruit is in blossom now
So come along, cuties, and shake the bough

ALL

By that goona goona goona lagoona lagoona lagoon.

> AS THE SIRENS CHARM THE UNWARY BOYS, A SAILOR CONKS
> ONE OF THEM OVER THE HEAD AND DRAGS HIM OFF. OTHERS
> SCAMPER INTO THE SHADOWS WITH THE GIGGLING SIRENS AS
> *ULYSSES* STANDS AGHAST. ONLY *DOC*, *ACHILLES* AND *BLUEY*
> *WIENERWITZ* ARE LEFT. *ULYSSES* REALIZES HIS FRIENDS ARE FAD-
> ING FAST. THE GARISH SET DRIFTS OFF AND THEY STAND IN
> EMPTY SPACE AGAIN.

THE THREE BOYS

Shanghaied!

ULYSSES, *bewildered*

Shanghaied!
This is one hell of a bender
These townfolks are mean as can be
  Of glory they've stripped us
  They've clipped us
                and gypped us
This is one *hell* of a spree!

THE THREE BOYS

Yessir, they sure fixed our wagons
Those wagons we hitched to a star
  We're not smart at all guys
  We're small guys
                And fall guys
We've stuck our necks out too far.

> *HECTOR* APPEARS, SMILING BLANDLY. AT THE SIGHT OF HIM
> *BLUEY* SHIVERS AND RUNS OFF. A TRIO OF SHIFTY CITIZENS

AWAIT HIM AND WHIRL HIM AWAY INTO THE DARKNESS.
ULYSSES, DOC AND ACHILLES ARE UNAWARE OF THIS AS THEY
WARILY TURN TO FACE HECTOR.

HECTOR

Here's a mind in a mix up, badly out of control
He's a hot bed of neuroses
He's a mass of conflicts, worried about his soul
He will need some sharp diagnoses

Ul YSSES

I don't trust your bright ideas
Your newfangled panaceas

HECTOR

Don't trust me, put your reliance
In the cold hard facts of science
It will free you from vain superstitions
From demons, taboos and angels with wings
It will shatter your antiquated traditions
Just hark to the hymn that the scientist sings!

A BURST OF RAGTIME. THE LIGHTS COME UP ON A FLAT PAINTED
WITH RHEOSTATS, DYNAMOS, RETORTS AND X-RAYS IN A TAN-
GLED PATTERN. A COMPLICATED ROCKET IN THE RUBE GOLDBERG
TRADITION OCCUPIES THE CENTER OF THE STAGE. TINKERING
WITH THE ROCKET IS LADY SCIENTIST (MISS MINERVA) IN A
SHORT SMOCK, BLOOMERS AND SHARP-TOED HIGH-LACED BOOTS.
SHE IS FLANKED BY TWO MALE ASSISTANTS, BLANK-FACED AS
ROBOTS. THEY ALL TURN TO FACE ULYSSES, DOC AND ACHILLES.
THE LADY SCIENTIST APPROACHES WITH QUICK, PRECISE LITTLE
STEPS.

THE LADY SCIENTIST

I've prodded the atom to its foundation
Cross-indexed the human mind
Reduced the universe to an equation

ULYSSES, DOC *and* ACHILLES

What oh what did you find?

THE LADY SCIENTIST, *cheerfully*

Oooo, the Polar Cap is slowly expanding
In a million years we'll freeze to death I guess
  If the Ice Age hasn't floored us
  There's a planet heading toward us
When it hits, we'll be an interstellar mess!

Oh our continent is crumbling and dissolving
As our rivers wash the topsoil out to sea
  And what land we can retrieve'll
  Be devoured by pest and weevil
And there won't be nothing left for you and me.

ALL

Oh we're doomed
Doomed, doomed
Oh we're doomed
Doomed, doomed
Oh we're doomed to disappear without a trace!

THE SCIENTIST

For our solar system's cracking up
The universe is slacking up

And time is running out
At a rather hectic pace!

ALL

Oh we're doomed
Doomed, doomed
Oh we're doomed
Doomed, doomed
Oh we're doomed to disappear without a trace!

THE SCIENTIST

Because all of us are just
Little specks of cosmic dust

ALL

Oh it's doom doom doom
For the well-known human race.

THE SCIENTIST

Once a man was the monarch of creation
Now he's just an unimportant carnivore
    For we've found in our researches
    His ingredients you can purchase
For a buck at your pharmacy store.

We're the accidental offspring of the monkeys
What a *better* breed a scientist could make
    For compared with all the glories
    Of our modern lab'ratories
Man is just a biological mistake!

ALL

Oh we're doomed
Doomed, doomed
Oh we're doomed
Doomed, doomed
Oh we're doomed to disappear without a trace!

THE SCIENTIST

For our solar system's cracking up
The universe is slacking up
And time is running out at a rather hectic pace.

ALL

Oh we're doomed
Doomed, doomed
Oh we're doomed
Doomed, doomed
Oh we're doomed to disappear without a trace

THE SCIENTIST

Because all of you are just
Little specks of cosmic dust

ALL

Oh it's doom doom doom
For the well-known human race!

> *THE SCIENTIST* GAILY DANCES BACK TO HER LABORATORY WHERE
> SHE FIDDLES WITH THE LEVERS OF THE HUGE GLISTENING
> ROCKET.

THE SCIENTIST

To save our all too human necks
I've now invented Gadget X.

ULYSSES

A gadget?

THE SCIENTIST, *complacently*

A *super* gadget!
Now just beyond the planet Mars
Is System Zero
Lots of stars
Aglow there

ULYSSES

We'll have to go there!

THE SCIENTIST

So when destruction starts to fall
Our Gadget X will save us all.

ULYSSES, DOC *and* ACHILLES

Hail gadget!

THE SCIENTIST

Hail *super* Gadget!

Oh it's effective, never fear
Now which of you will volunteer
To ride it?
I've never tried it.

DOC

I will be the volunteer!

ALL

He will be the volunteer!

THEY RUSH HIM TO THE BACK AND PUT HIM INTO THE MACHINE. *THE SCIENTIST* PULLS A SWITCH. A TREMENDOUS FLASH, AND THE ROCKET FLIES OFF INTO SPACE. *THE SCIENTIST* IS WILD WITH DELIGHT.

THE SCIENTIST, *joyously*

It works! It works!
He's plunging past time's track
In twenty seconds flat

ULYSSES

But how is he gonna get back?

THE SCIENTIST

Oh dear! oh dear!
I never thought of that.

Well, back to work!

WITH A SHRUG OF HER SHOULDERS SHE AND HER ASSISTANTS MARCH BACK INTO THE LABORATORY, WHICH BLACKS OUT.

ULYSSES

Enough is enough
The game is played out
And all of our pals
Have pulled a fade-out!

HECTOR COMES FORWARD. *ULYSSES*, VERY ANGRY, GRABS HIM BY THE LAPELS.

I'm wise to this joint now
It's fight or get beaten
I get the point now
It's eat or be eaten.

HECTOR, WHO HAS BEEN VERY CALM DURING *ULYSSES'* TIRADE,
INSOLENTLY PUSHES HIM AWAY. AS *HECTOR* SINGS, THE CITY
REAPPEARS AT THE BACK. THE STAGE IS SLOWLY PEOPLED BY
FIGURES SUGGESTING THE SUBTLE AND/OR SQUALID NIGHT LIFE
OF RHODODENDRON. THE CITY, THE SKY AND THE PEOPLE HAVE
A COLD, SINISTER QUALITY, UTTERLY DIFFERENT FROM THE PRE-
VIOUS VIEW WE HAD OF IT

HECTOR

On the wrong side of the tracks
Where the city's white lights turn red
Lives a lady known as Circe
Who fills good folks' hearts with dread

Oh the magic she can spin
Makes a shiver run up your spine
She turns water into gin
And she turns men into swine

THE NIGHT PEOPLE
Circe, Circe
The woman without mercy
Circe turns men into swine.

CIRCE APPEARS IN A FLASH, LIKE A LADY IN A MAGICIAN'S ACT,
ON THE TOP OF THE SKYLINE. BECAUSE OF THE PERSPECTIVE OF
THE BUILDINGS SHE SEEMS TO TOWER LIKE AN UNDULANT
GIANTESS OVER THE CITY. SHE WEARS BLACK AND SHE IS COV-

ERED WITH A FLOATING VEIL GLITTERING WITH STARS. AS SHE
WALKS DOWN OVER THE ROOFTOPS WHICH BECOME STAIRS FOR
HER FEET, SHE SLOWLY RAISES THE VEIL AND WE SEE THAT IT
IS *PENELOPE* TRANSFORMED.

(*CIRCE* DOES NOT SUGGEST LURID SEX IN THE SENSE THAT THE
SIRENS HAVE. HERE, THE EFFECT IS A TOTAL ONE—DOMINATION
OVER EVERYTHING THAT HAS BEEN PUSHING *ULYSSES* AROUND
IS OFFERED TO HIM. IN ORDER TO SECURE THIS HE MUST GIVE
UP WHAT IS MOST TENDER AND MOST ALIVE IN HIMSELF. THAT
IS WHY *PENELOPE* IS USED TO REPRESENT *CIRCE*.)

PARIS APPEARS AND THROUGHOUT THE SCENE HE DOES A DANCE
OF LONGING FOR *CIRCE*, WHO IS INDIFFERENT TO HIM AND
ATTENTIVE TO *ULYSSES*.

HECTOR

She's the city when it's evil
In her veins flows rock and rye
You had better hide in a doorway
When you see her passing by

She's got night-colored hair
Shiny eyes like two full moons
And her laughter's like an echo
Of the honky-tonk saloons.

CIRCE RELEASES HER VEIL. SOME OF THE NIGHT PEOPLE SEIZE
IT AS IT FALLS AND RUN AWAY, TEARING AND TUGGING AT IT
AMONG THEMSELVES. *ULYSSES* MOVES TOWARD HER, EVADING
THE OUTSTRETCHED HAND OF *ACHILLES*.

CIRCE

I was born exactly at midnight
And I grew up by half-past two
If I move too fast for comfort
Maybe I'll slow down for you

From sundown to sunrise
I'm available for a fee
I take a world that's mean and dingy
Make it glitter like a Christmas tree

THE NIGHT PEOPLE, *softly*

Circe, Circe
The woman without mercy
Circe turns men into swine.

HECTOR

Ulysses, we've mystified you
Oh we've tried to drag you down
But, boy, with this gal beside you
You can rule this doggone town

ULYSSES TRIES TO TOUCH THE ELUSIVE CIRCE. PARIS RETREATS TO
THE CORNER OF THE STAGE WHERE HECTOR WAITS, SMILING.
ACHILLES MOVES BETWEEN ULYSSES AND CIRCE.

ACHILLES

If you're gonna care for Circe
Then you'd better trim your sails
'Cause she's gonna scratch your heart out
With her long red fingernails

ULYSSES

It's much wiser to be heartless
For a heart is a hazard, I learn
If I give you mine, Madame Circe
What do I get in return?

CIRCE

There are just two kinds of people
Those who follow and those who lead
I will make you so cold and clever
You'll be certain to succeed

THE NIGHT PEOPLE

Circe, Circe
The woman without mercy
Circe turns men into swine.

ULYSSES AND CIRCE WEAVE SLOWLY AMONG THE DANCING NIGHT PEOPLE. HECTOR MOTIONS TO ONE OF THE NIGHT PEOPLE, WHO GIVES HIM A KNIFE. HECTOR SNAPS IT OPEN AND GIVES IT TO PARIS.

HECTOR, *secretly*

Paris!
This is all your doin
'Cause you went wooin

You dragged that fool in
And now he's rulin

But we all hate him
So liquidate him

And Circe will love you.

PARIS REFUSES AND TURNS AWAY, BUT HECTOR HOLDS HIM BY
THE ARM. THE FOCUS OF ATTENTION SHIFTS BACK TO ULYSSES
AND CIRCE AS THE NIGHT PEOPLE RECEDE INTO THE SHADOWS.

ULYSSES

Love will last for an hour
Be it false or be it true
But what can you give me
That will last me all life through?

CIRCE

Love will last for an hour
Be it weak or be it strong
But I will give you power
That will last you all life long

THE NIGHT PEOPLE

Circe, Circe
The woman without mercy
Circe turns men into swine.

CIRCE SUDDENLY TURNS AND HOLDS OUT THE GOLDEN APPLE
WE HAVE SEEN IN THE FIRST ACT. THE NIGHT PEOPLE SWARM
OUT OF THE SHADOWS AND GRASP AT IT. ULYSSES ACCEPTS IT
AND LINKS HIS ARM IN CIRCE'S. PARIS AND THE CROWD WHIRL
ABOUT, TENSE WITH ENVY AND GREED. HECTOR AGAIN SNAPS
OPEN THE KNIFE AND OFFERS IT TO PARIS, WHO TAKES IT.
CIRCE IS LEADING ULYSSES UP THE LEVEL TO THE ROOFTOPS SO
HIS BACK IS AN EASY TARGET.

PARIS, WITH THE EXCITED STEALTH OF THE MUGGER, APPROACHES *ULYSSES* TO STAB HIM, BUT *ACHILLES* SEES HIM, CALLS OUT TO *ULYSSES* AND INTERCEPTS THE BLOW. AS *ULYSSES* TURNS, *ACHILLES* STAGGERS TO HIM AND DROPS DEAD AT HIS FEET. *ULYSSES* BENDS OVER THE BODY OF HIS FRIEND AS THE NIGHT PEOPLE, SNICKERING AND EXULTANT, SCURRY OFF INTO THE DOORWAYS AND ALLEYS OF THE TOWN. *ULYSSES* LOOKS UP TO SEE *CIRCE* AND *PARIS* RUNNING OVER THE ROOFTOPS TOGETHER.

(NOTE: THIS SCENE ESPECIALLY—AS INDEED, ALL THE OTHERS— MUST NOT BE DONE WITH ANY PRETENTIOUS AIR OF SYMBOLISM OR STYLISTIC ABSTRACTION. IT SHOULD HAVE THE ATMOSPHERE OF THE LAST STAGES OF A BENDER, WHEN EVERYTHING HAS A DISCONNECTED CLARITY THAT IS COMPLETELY CONFUSING. IF ANY STYLE IS INDICATED HERE, IT IS THAT OF THE TEN'-TWENT'- THIRT' MELODRAMA, ALTHOUGH IT SHOULD NOT BE CARRIED OVER INTO THE AREA OF COMIC BURLESQUE.)

HECTOR AND *ULYSSES* ARE LEFT ALONE ON STAGE WITH THE BODY OF *ACHILLES. HECTOR* LOOKS AT *ULYSSES* ALMOST WITH AN AIR OF AFFECTION.

HECTOR, feelingly

It was grand
Really grand
To have known you
And all of your wonderful crew
But you've lost the friends you've known
And at last you're on your own
And it's certain to be curtains for you too.

HE WALKS AWAY OVER THE ROOFTOPS SLOWLY, DISAPPEARING OVER THE EDGE WITHOUT A BACKWARD GLANCE. *ULYSSES* THROWS THE APPLE FROM HIM. THE LIGHTS SHIFT AND THE ILLUSION OF THE CITY BEGINS TO DIM. A STARRY DROP DE- SCENDS OVER THE BLACK OUTLINE OF THE CITY.

ONE OF THE BUILDINGS BECOMES TRANSPARENT ENOUGH FOR US TO SEE *MOTHER HARE*, SWATHED IN A DARK CLOAK SO THAT SHE SEEMS TO FLOAT IN SPACE. SHE HOLDS THE GOLDEN APPLE IN HER HAND. BEHIND HER IS A CHORUS, ALSO IN BLACK CLOAKS.

ULYSSES SPEAKS ALOUD, HIS QUESTIONS ADDRESSED TO HIMSELF, NOT TO THE AUDIENCE. HE REACTS TO THE MUSICAL ECHOES OF *MOTHER HARE* AND THE CHORUS AS IF THEY WERE ANSWERS TO HIS QUESTIONS.

ULYSSES

Despair cuts through me like a knife
What is the meaning of life?

MOTHER HARE

Life

ULYSSES

So short a time Man draws his breath
Then what is the mystery of death?

MOTHER HARE

Death

ULYSSES

Since life and death go hand in glove
What motive has a man to love?

MOTHER HARE

Love

ULYSSES

When love becomes a mocking wraith
Then what leads the anxious heart to faith?

CHORUS

Faith

ULYSSES

As through dear darkened lives we grope
What reason has a man to hope?

CHORUS

Hope

ULYSSES

We vainly follow Hope's pale gleam
Then what keeps the dreamer from his dream?

CHORUS

His dream

THE CITY FADES. THE STAGE SLOWLY STARTS TO BRIGHTEN.
ULYSSES ASSUMES THE ASSURANCE OF A PERSON WHO HAS
FOUND AN INTERIOR ANSWER TO HIS QUESTIONS.

ULYSSES

Yes life is life's answer
And death is the same
Love, faith, hope and dreams
All the things I can name
All answer themselves

Together, not apart
In the unspoken wisdom
Of the living heart.

I know that I am myself
And I am also other men
And knowing this truly
I can go home again

I can go home again.

THE LIGHTS DIM ON HIM. THE CURTAINS PART TO SHOW THE
BACK YARD OF *PENELOPE'S* HOUSE IN ANGEL'S ROOST. A WHITE
FENCE CROSSES THE BACK OF THE STAGE, GARLANDED WITH
MORNING GLORIES. *MISS MINERVA, MRS. JUNIPER* AND *LOVEY
MARS* SIT GROUPED ABOUT *PENELOPE. MOTHER HARE,* TO ONE
SIDE, STITCHES ON A PIECE OF BLACK CREPE. *MENELAUS* LIES
AT *HELEN'S* FEET AS SHE WINDS WOOL AROUND HIS HANDS.

PENELOPE IS BUSILY AT WORK ON HER QUILT. THE TEN YEARS
THAT HAVE PASSED ARE SHOWN IN THE STYLES WORN BY THE
LADIES AS THEY LIVEN UP THE SEWING BEE BY GOING OVER A
SUBJECT THEY HAVE OBVIOUSLY COVERED MANY TIMES BEFORE.

LADIES

Buzz buzz
Buzz buzz
Busy little sewing bee
Where's your fellow
Poor Penelope?
It's ten years since he went away
I'll bet he's dead and under clay
If not where is he?
(Busy little sewing bee)

PENELOPE SMILES AND HOLDS UP HER PATCHWORK QUILT FOR
INSPECTION. SHE POINTS TO EACH SCRAP AS SHE ITEMIZES IT.

PENELOPE

Somehow I keep believing
That he'll return one day
Into this quilt I'm weaving
Our life that went astray
This bit of faded cotton
Is from his working shirt
And I'd almost forgotten
This silk from my Sunday skirt
Here's a scrap of ribbon
I borrowed to wear on the day we wed
Here's a square of linen
From the pillow of our marriage bed

LADIES, *interrupting*

Where's Ulysses
Lord Almighty, where is he?
What's Ulysses? Nothing but a memory
Ten years back he left board and bed
And legally you're free to wed
Don't act so dizzy!
(Busy little sewing bee)

HELEN

It's a lazy afternoon
Why do you sit there a stitching
When you're free to be bewitching
All those eager beaux who're itching

To woo
Lucky you

MENELAUS, *striking a pose like* PARIS

It's a lazy afternoon
Why sit here and ply your needle
As your boy friends beg and wheedle
Is it wise to let them tweedle
    Their thumbs
    Till he comes?

LADIES

Buzz buzz
Buzz buzz
Busy little sewing bee
Choose a feller
Poor Penelope

PENELOPE, *gently insistent*

I vowed I would not choose before
I finished up my sewing chore

LADIES, *gossiping*

We're in a tizzy
Busy little sewing bee.

FOUR SUITORS FOLLOWED BY FOUR UNMARRIED MAIDENS ENTER
TO WOO *PENELOPE.*

THE FOUR SUITORS

Penelope say whichaway
You'll give your love and beauty

Don't just sit there and stitch away
And blame it all on duty!

THE MAIDENS

While you wait for that gadabout
That no-good faithless cuss
You've cornered every lad about
There's no one left for us!

PENELOPE

This quilt of mine displays his love
A love of shining beauty

MOTHER HARE, *behind her*

He's pushing up the daisies, love
So let him go to blazes, love
And don't be so darned snooty
Go pick another cutie.

> SHE PULLS THE QUILT OUT OF *PENELOPE'S* HANDS. THE GIRLS
> TOSS IT UP LIKE A DANCING VEIL AS *PENELOPE*, LAUGHING,
> TRIES TO RETRIEVE IT.

THE SUITORS, *reprovingly*

Penelope, you're frivolous
We have no time to lose
The next ten years may shrivel us
The time has come to choose!

PENELOPE, *counting out*

Eeny, Meeny, Miney, Mo
Whichaway shall my heart go?
The Parson, Banker Carson,
The Smith or Farmer Joe?

THE FLOAT SUDDENLY EMERGES FROM THE WINGS, BATTERED,
TATTERED AND DISHEVELED. *ULYSSES* IS ALONE IN THE STERN.
THE FIGUREHEAD IS BAREFOOT, HER CROWN ASKEW, HER GOWN
RAGGED. SHE SAGS OVER, EXHAUSTED.

THE FIGUREHEAD, *wearily*

Row boy, row
Row up the river
All aboard all aboard
That are coming with me

ULYSSES *and* THE FIGUREHEAD

Whichaway Whichaway
Does that old red river run?

From Rhododendron
To the setting sun

From Rhododendron
To the setting sun.

ULYSSES LEAPS OFF THE FLOAT. IT STAGGERS OFF. HE RUNS
TOWARD *PENELOPE. HELEN* INDIGNANTLY INTERRUPTS HIM—RE-
FORMED, SHE IS NOW A PILLAR OF LOCAL VIRTUE.

HELEN

He leaves you flat
Then has the gall
To show his face back here!

Penelope
Don't let him stall
Be tough on him, dear!

He drinks and gambles
And rambles
Then back to home he ambles
Throw him out on his ear!

OTHER LADIES

Uh *huh*
Throw him right out on his ear!

PENELOPE STANDS QUIETLY AS ULYSSES APPROACHES. WHEN
HE TRIES TO EMBRACE HER SHE PUSHES HIM AWAY VIOLENTLY.
HE IS TAKEN BY SURPRISE. THE OTHERS TIPTOE AWAY.

PENELOPE, *caustic*

Oh it's you back, is it?
Are you home for a visit?
  Wipe your feet on the mat
  And hang up your hat
And ask for a change of clothes?

Should I roll out a carpet
Ask you sweetly how you are, pet?
  As you sit and chat?

And after that
Away you'll scat
To follow your foolish nose
Whichaway the next wind blows?

What did you expect?
That I'd just stay put
Tapping my foot
Refusing to cut up
Till you strut up
  To my consternation.

What did you expect?
That I'd be real prim
Happy to trim
The lamp in my window
  Living in domestic isolation?

Well you're wrong, Ulysses
Ulysses, you're wrong!
I got along without you
So you had better get along, too!

SHE BURIES HER FACE IN HER HANDS. *ULYSSES* LOOKS DOWN
AT THE CHAIR AND SEES THE QUILT, RECOGNIZING WHAT THE
BITS AND PIECES REPRESENT. HE HOLDS IT OUT TO HER
BESEECHINGLY.

ULYSSES, *softly*

Penelope, my dear,
The pieces are all still here
The years blow away

Lightly as a feather
But see
Everything still holds together

PENELOPE, *sadly*

What can we do?
Let your heart be truthful
What can we do
To renew our joy?

Look at us two
I am not so youthful
You're not a starry-eyed
Impetuous boy.

Why did you go away
And leave me all alone?

ULYSSES, *with persuasive male logic*

If I had never gone away
I never could come home to stay
The certainty for which I yearned
Was waiting here when I returned

Here between your outstretched hands
Are all my magic distant lands
Here in your familiar eyes
Is all the wisdom of the wise

SHE TAKES THE QUILT FROM HIM AND FOLDS IT CAREFULLY.
ULYSSES HOLDS HER CLOSE.

ULYSSES

It's the coming home together
When your work is through
Someone asks you How de do
    And How'd it go today?

It's the knowing someone's there
When you climb up the stair
Who always seems to know
    All the things you're gonna say.

PENELOPE YIELDS TO HIM. THE REST OF THE CAST SLOWLY ENTERS
DURING THE FOLLOWING REPRISE, FORMING A GLOWING TAB-
LEAU AS THE SHOW MOVES TO ITS FINALE.

PENELOPE *and* ULYSSES

It's the being home together
When the shadows rise
Someone looks into your eyes
    And takes you by the hand

It's a dear familiar face
That can light up a place
And little private jokes
    Only you two understand

ALL

It's the going home together
Through the changing years
It's the talk about the weather
And the laughter and the tears

PENELOPE *and* ULYSSES

It's to love the you that's me
And the me that's you

ALL

It's the going home together
All life through!

THE SKY IS BATHED IN A CLEAR YELLOW LIGHT. *ULYSSES* AND
PENELOPE MOVE UP THE STAIRS OF THEIR HOUSE AS

THE CURTAIN FALLS

THE GOLDEN APPLE

CAST OF CHARACTERS

HELEN : Mezzo-Soprano

MOTHER HARE. : Contralto

MRS. JUNIPER : Mezzo-Soprano

PENELOPE : Soprano

MISS MINERVA OLIVER : Soprano

LOVEY MARS : Contralto

PARIS : Dancer

MENELAUS : Tenor

ULYSSES : Baritone

HECTOR CHARYBDIS : Bass

SIX HEROES (Singers)
    PATROCLUS : Tenor
    DIOMEDE : Tenor
    DOC MACCAHAN : Tenor
    ACHILLES : Baritone
    AJAX : Bass-Baritone
    NESTOR : Bass

SIX HEROES (Dancers)
    MARS, AGAMEMNON, BLUEY, THIRSTY, SILAS, HOMER

SIX GIRL DANCERS

SINGING CHORUS
Four Sopranos
Four Altos (1 The Figurehead)
Four Tenors
Four Basses